Becoming a CHRISTIAN COUNSELLOR

A PATHWAY TOWARDS EXCELLENCE
IN PSYCHOTHERAPY

TREVOR R. SUMMERLIN

WESTBOW
PRESS®
A DIVISION OF THOMAS NELSON
& ZONDERVAN

Copyright © 2021 Trevor R. Summerlin.

All rights reserved. No part of this book may be used or reproduced by any means, graphic, electronic, or mechanical, including photocopying, recording, taping or by any information storage retrieval system without the written permission of the author except in the case of brief quotations embodied in critical articles and reviews.

This book is a work of non-fiction. Unless otherwise noted, the author and the publisher make no explicit guarantees as to the accuracy of the information contained in this book and in some cases, names of people and places have been altered to protect their privacy.

WestBow Press books may be ordered through booksellers or by contacting:

WestBow Press
A Division of Thomas Nelson & Zondervan
1663 Liberty Drive
Bloomington, IN 47403
www.westbowpress.com
844-714-3454

Because of the dynamic nature of the Internet, any web addresses or links contained in this book may have changed since publication and may no longer be valid. The views expressed in this work are solely those of the author and do not necessarily reflect the views of the publisher, and the publisher hereby disclaims any responsibility for them.

Any people depicted in stock imagery provided by Getty Images are models, and such images are being used for illustrative purposes only. Certain stock imagery © Getty Images.

Scripture quotations taken from The Holy Bible, New International Version® NIV® Copyright © 1973 1978 1984 2011 by Biblica, Inc. TM. Used by permission. All rights reserved worldwide.

Interior Image Credit: Trevor R. Summerlin

ISBN: 978-1-6642-3993-7 (sc)
ISBN: 978-1-6642-3992-0 (e)

Print information available on the last page.

WestBow Press rev. date: 08/04/2021

FOREWORD

This book introduces the reader to the traditional major secular psychological approaches to counselling and psychotherapy, it focuses on, defines and clarifies what constitutes Christian counselling and also describes what it is not. It makes a valuable contribution by relating how some of the elements of these secular approaches can contribute to the principles of Christianity. Trevor comments on the lack of understanding of the whole concept of Christian counselling as something which he has continuously encountered. In his introduction, he describes the struggles he has observed church leaders experiencing when trying to maintain a programme of Christian counselling and comments on the need to prioritise the development of a counselling team. He considers the confusion around the role of a counsellor and how it is understood by church leaders, the idea that arises amongst church leaders that secular psychology has no place in the church, and also the need of some leaders to exercise control in these matters. His considered opinion that everything in psychological therapy only works if it is in line with the way God has designed us is explored in detail, while emphasising that ignoring the spiritual dimension is not likely to allow any of a person's real issues to be addressed.

The chapter layout is clear and begins with a definition of the terms used. It is followed by some personal revelations and what is referred to as the Christian prerogative. A comprehensive explanation of each of the major psychological approaches and their history follows: The Person Centred approach, the Existential approach, the Psychodynamic approach, the Cognitive Behavioural approach together with Motivational Interviewing. Various models of Christian counselling are clearly described, other forms of Christian helping are reviewed and the Waverley Model with its five elements is explored in some detail.

The safety of the therapeutic environment together with issues of boundaries, confidentiality and privacy is explored throughout the book. Acknowledging the importance of recognising the whole person and also that the only expert in any person's life is the person themself is stressed, a concept introduced by Carl Rogers which challenged the role of the professional expert at the time. A non directive approach is emphasised, including the importance of building trust and respect for client autonomy together with the necessity to demonstrate the core conditions of empathy, genuineness and unconditional positive regard, without which there will be an inappropriate power imbalance. Within the safety of this contracted therapeutic environment the client can gain confidence and insight, consider changes, develop their problem solving skills, set goals, consider their support systems and make autonomous decisions, helping them to grow and flourish, which all contribute to building their resilience. The recognition of the impact of childhood experiences which are often the root causes of behaviour in the individual's development, are also noted.

Trevor's experience in counselling and lecturing spans over forty years and his enthusiasm for "the potential of counselling and how it is best done from a Christian perspective" is evident and this together with his knowledge and experience contributes to a balanced and insightful book. Recognising that there is much poor quality counselling being offered, he describes the qualities Christian counsellors should aspire to and the criteria or standards by which people could be considered to be Christian counsellors.

I believe the book makes an important contribution to Christian counselling literature as it describes what it means to be a Christian psychotherapist and explains both Christian and secular approaches, clarifying any confusion that may arise between the two. As the title suggests it is aimed at those considering becoming a Christian counsellor although I think that it is an excellent source of knowledge and insight both for the Christian and the secular counsellor, the newly trained and the experienced counsellor and for all church leaders. I believe the book does what it sets out to do "to establish a clear rationale for counselling" and it describes a pathway towards excellence in psychotherapy while acknowledging that all true wisdom comes only from God.

I was both surprised and delighted to receive an email in the middle of a dark wintry national lockdown asking me to write a foreword for this book. I replied that I was honoured to be asked. Trevor was my first tutor in counselling and a lecturing colleague. Inspired by my introduction to counselling I proceeded to study further and pursued my interest in counselling children and young people by achieving a Masters degree in this field. I went on to complete a Post Graduate Diploma in Systemic Counselling and a Post Graduate Diploma in Supervision. I currently counsel both adults and children and supervise counsellors.

Delena Ritter BA, MA, PGDip. Counselling, PG Dip.
Systemic Counselling, PGDip. Supervision

ACKNOWLEDGEMENTS

I am deeply indebted to Rev. Selwyn Hughes who was the founder of the Crusade for World Revival (CWR), and to Rev. Trevor Partridge his colleague at the time. Selwyn developed the 5 Circle Model for Christian Counselling and it was this that completely revolutionised my whole understanding of counselling when I attended his Institute in Christian Counselling in May 1990 at Waverley Abbey. Learning about this model confirmed to me my calling as a Christian Counsellor and I have chosen to make it an integral part of every aspect of my work since that time. Much later it has become widely recognised and taught as The Waverley Model.

I am particularly grateful to Jane Wyatt, head of the counselling department, and to Theresa Chakravorty, at Cardiff and Vale College (formerly Barry College) in South Wales, UK. They taught me so much about the field of Existential counselling and consistently modelled the highest principles of how to be a good lecturer, tutor and counsellor.

There is a large number of other people who, over the years, have been instrumental in my development as a counsellor and psychotherapist, but regrettably I am only able to pay tribute to a few of them here. In particular I want to thank Thea James, Robert Lewis, Carol Moss and Fred Olsen who were some of my tutors on the Counselling Diploma at Gwent College in the early 1990's, and Dr Kathy Sherrod, a Christian psychologist from USA who was such an inspiration to me. I am also grateful to Frank Wells, my tutor at the University of Wales who gave me such a clear understanding of the practice of Cognitive therapy, and to my fellow students who gave me much needed motivation and focus throughout that pioneering course.

There is a vast number of additional people I am unable to thank who, over many years, have trusted me to be their counsellor. They will never know just how much they have all helped to shape and develop the way I work today, but I am extremely grateful to all of them. Similarly, all the students with whom I have been privileged to act as a lecturer and tutor have also played a vital part in the continuing development of my practice. I am grateful too, to all the agencies, centres and companies that have allowed me to work as a counsellor with their clients. They have all contributed to my understanding of what it means to be effective as a counsellor. I am grateful also to my fellow tutors and lecturers who have been a constant source of inspiration and to the counsellors who have trusted me to be their supervisor, from whom I have learned and continue to learn so much.

My special thanks go to my life-long friend and mentor Rev John James and his wife Trish for their on-going encouragement and inspiration in many ways which they may never realise, and to my wife Jan, who has had to endure endless periods when I've been counselling, supervising, preparing, teaching, training, marking, studying, researching or writing. I would not have been able to maintain my focus in any of these areas without her. Finally, I am totally amazed at the incredible empowering of God's Holy Spirit who opened to me this whole new opportunity for writing when I wasn't looking for it, and without whom none of this would have been possible.

CONTENTS

Foreword..v
Acknowledgements.. ix
Introduction..xv

1   Understanding the Terminology 1
2   Personal Revelations... 12
3   The Christian Prerogative 18
4   Person-Centred Therapy 24
5   The Existential Approach.. 36
6   The Psychodynamic Approach 44
7   The Cognitive Behavioural Approach 53
8   Motivational Interviewing... 63
9   Various Christian Approaches to Counselling 74
10 How does Christian Counselling Compare with Other
    Forms of Christian Helping ? 86
11 The Waverley Model 100
12 Conclusions.. 124

Appendices..131
References and Bibliography..141
About the Author...145
Other Publications by the same author..147

Please note that throughout this book whenever the words 'he', 'him', 'his', 'she', or 'her', have been used, no gender preference is intended.

FIGURES

Fig 1. The Four Dimensions of Life 37
Fig 2. The Purpose of Empathy 55
Fig 3. The Cognitive Case Formulation 58
Fig 4. The Stages of Change Model 65
Fig 5. The Five Circle Model 102
Fig 6. The 10 Basic Life Areas 105
Fig 7. The Roman Road 114
Fig 8. An example of a prayer of confession and repentance 116
Fig 9. "Before and After" 118
Fig 10. The Five Elements in Total Harmony 123

INTRODUCTION

For many years, as a Christian, I had been offering, what I considered to be counselling, to people who were experiencing some kind of difficulty in their life. It wasn't until I attended the "Institute in Christian Counselling" run by Selwyn Hughes at Waverley Abbey in 1990 that I became really fired up about the whole potential of counselling and how the very best way of doing this, by far, is from a Christian perspective. It was through this programme God, through Selwyn, revealed to me the enormous opportunities we have as Christians to help people identify the root of their problems and then help them explore ways of dealing with any blockages they may have that are preventing them from moving towards achieving real satisfaction and fulfilment in life. For the first time I realised that Christian Counselling can offer this prospect in a way that no other psychological approach ever can.

I was so excited about this concept that I felt every church should be offering Christian counselling, not simply to their members but especially to the wider community in which they are situated. Since that time I have taught scores of Christian counselling courses, been involved in dozens of attempts to establish Christian counselling teams in local communities and worked with lots of individual churches, but they have all struggled to maintain a programme of Christian Counselling. Of course, there will be many contributory factors as to why this has been the case, but I have been especially concerned about one aspect in particular – people do not seem to understand what actually constitutes Christian counselling - and this creates a major problem for many ministers and church leaders as well as the public at large. It is quite common for those in church leadership to believe it is solely their own prerogative to provide any and all counselling that maybe required, whether they have received any formal training for this or not, and many non-church people view with a great deal of suspicion any form of counselling which might have the slightest hint of a Christian emphasis attached to it.

Unfortunately it is quite possible for those in leadership to confuse the task of being an educator of people in the teachings of scripture, with the role of being a counsellor. The majority of ministerial training organisations now include a short module about counselling and then give their students the impression they are now qualified in this area of ministry. However, counsellors currently require a minimum of four years (part time) training to reach an acceptable level of qualification, whereas some ministers see counselling simply as a disciplinary measure that can be applied to any aspects of misconduct with their church members. A much more serious concern however, is the need for leaders to think they should know everything that is going on, and the belief that they should have sole responsibility for handling all the struggles in which any of their members are engaged. Furthermore, they can develop a real fear about not knowing, which can create resentment towards those who may be working as qualified counsellors. This smacks of a controlling mentality and speaks more about the weaknesses of the leaders than of their genuine concerns about the wellbeing of their members.

Possibly the greatest benefit to ministers, pastors and church leaders of having a team of qualified counsellors in their church, and one that is frequently overlooked, is their willingness to spend time with people who are struggling to manage some difficulty in their lives and seem unable to find a way forward. The counsellor is able to take his time helping each person get to the source of their issues rather than give a quick or dismissive answer. It is often the volume of people who need in-depth help that puts unnecessary pressure onto ministers and which can dramatically increase their levels of stress. The knowledge that counsellors will work in a structured, systematic manner which supports people as they seek to come to terms with their issues, can be a real asset to any church leader and can create a great deal of freedom for them to spend time elsewhere.

This raises an issue over which there is a great deal of confusion in the Christian church generally, the application of confidentiality. Counsellors learn the necessity of this at an early stage in their training, and it includes developing a clear understanding of the circumstances under which confidentiality should be broken. Church people often seem to be baffled by the difference between confidentiality and privacy, or recognising what is private and what it is appropriate to share with others. Whenever anyone gets this wrong it can cause a large amount of hurt, distress and distrust amongst people, and what is being modelled to others soon becomes general practice for everybody in the organisation. As a result of this, people will often make the choice to not seek help from folk within the church, preferring instead to either let their issues remain buried beneath the surface or seek help from a secular source.

Another element that often surfaces among church leaders is the concern that secular psychology has no place in the church because The Bible, with the inspiration of The Holy Spirit, provides everything that is ever likely to be needed. They see a conflict here which actually doesn't exist. It is similar to the conflict which might be imagined between the skills of a qualified doctor against the healing power of The Holy Spirit. Both are able to work in perfect harmony. Whilst The Bible gives us a clear picture of God's practical plans and purposes for us, it doesn't involve turning our backs on people who are trained and qualified in the specialist fields for which God has gifted them. For example, it teaches us that God wants us to prosper and be successful in business but it doesn't say exactly who we should trust or where we should advertise our services. Being willing to learn from non-spiritual people does not mean that we have to accept everything they say. We must learn to be prayerfully selective in such matters because we believe in the absolute sovereignty of God and that all true wisdom comes only from Him. So to dismiss the amazing advances in the understandings of human psychology is sheer foolishness provided that, in accepting these, we do not sacrifice our faith and trust in the person of Jesus, our risen saviour, and we do not accept anything that contradicts The Word of God.

If we are to accept counselling as a valid Christian ministry, it is essential that we do not simply allow just anyone to be involved with it, nor think that all we need is for The Holy Spirit to give us all the answers. We should apply the same reasoning to those we invite to preach and teach or lead worship in our churches. God's whole strategy is for every person to use their God-given ability to make their own discoveries and choices in the light of His Word and then to receive comprehensive training and equipping to minister their gifts to others. We must recognise that some of the people who will feel drawn towards becoming counsellors will not have the right qualities of character to take on such a role. This emphasises one of the major reasons for people to undertake formal counselling training. There is a sense in which God is committed to use the natural gifts He has deposited within us but that usually means we must take the responsibility to get whatever training is necessary to develop these in order to be able to use them appropriately.

One difficulty that frequently occurs in churches is that the people who are the most naturally suitable and gifted with regard to offering counselling are often already heavily committed in other aspects of family and church work and are therefore unable to devote sufficient time to additional training. To develop a church counselling team, like developing a worship team or an evangelistic team, will require the leadership to make it a priority so that the most gifted people can be freed up from some of their other commitments.

It is most important for everyone to be taught what we mean when we use the term 'Counselling' and how this is different from other forms of Christian helping and ministry. There is so much poor quality counselling being offered today that it is quite easy for people to develop a jaundiced view of the potential benefits. Not only are there plenty of poor, inadequately trained people who want to call themselves counsellors, but there are a myriad of psychologically suspect and dubious approaches being talked about as 'therapy'. There is a massive growth taking place in the number of people who call themselves therapists and this is, I believe, very largely due to the fact that Christians have not seen it as their prerogative to meet the demands of the public in this respect and have consequently left a huge gap in the market.

Counselling does not obviate the need for other Christian ministries, and we will look at some of these later in the book but, unless we understand how they can all fit together whilst offering something quite different, there will always be a great deal of confusion in the church about the need for counselling, the role of counselling, and who should be providing counselling. My intention in this book is to convince people of the huge benefits of an approach to counselling which is totally in line with the teachings of The Bible and that this is not only a possibility but is actually the responsibility of Christian believers. I want to dispel some of the myths about Christian counselling, I want to help people overcome a lack of understanding about some of the major psychological approaches, and to resist the temptation to 'throw the baby out with the bathwater'. I also want to encourage many more Christians to see the benefits of choosing to undertake formal counsellor training to become qualified and recognised by the world at large. In this way, Christian churches could make a phenomenal difference in the communities wherever they are situated.

I am aware that Christian counsellors may need to work in a wide variety of different settings and therefore the requirements placed upon them may also vary greatly. Even though I have chosen to write from the perspective of someone working in private practice, I recognise that this may still include the need to receive referrals from a mixture of different sources, many of which may not be sympathetic to the Christian approach. This raises the question of how a Christian counsellor can work with non-believers, or people of other faiths. The answer is, I believe, quite simply that the Christian counsellor is interested in every aspect of a person's life which might interfere with their ability to live in the way God intended, whether they believe this or not. God never intended anyone to deal with every issue in life entirely on their own. We all need the help of someone else on occasions and consulting a Christian counsellor is an excellent place to start. I believe it is perfectly possible for a Christian counsellor to work ethically and honourably with every person who requests their help without compromising their faith in any way and without pressurising their clients to accept what they themselves believe. I hope this book will demonstrate a pathway through which this can be achieved.

There are literally hundreds of different theories and psychological approaches to counselling, many of which are simply variations of interpretation of some of the well established theories. Nevertheless, it can be helpful to understand a little of how some of them emphasise different aspects of the personality and how these elements relate to the principles of Christianity. The book begins with an attempt to avoid any ambiguity by establishing a clear understanding of the terminology I have used. I have then chosen to follow a progression of what I consider to be the most helpful aspects of some of the major psychological approaches and how these can add to our understanding of what it means to be a Christian Psychotherapist. It is not possible to go into great detail about each one of these but this is intended to whet the appetite and act as an encouragement to explore them further. The latter part of the book is an in-depth study into the practical application of the Waverley Christian Model showing how this can be used with clients from every conceivable background regardless of whether they have any faith or not. The book concludes with a range of materials and tools which I hope will be of practical help to those who wish to develop as a Christian counsellor.

I do not approach the writing of this book from the position of being an expert in this field but as someone who has been learning for over 40 years now and is still struggling to learn how to grow and develop in the art of helping people effectively. I believe that a good counsellor will never get to the position where he feels he has no more to learn and will never be taken by surprise as new ways of working with the human personality continue to emerge. He will also recognise that the only expert in any person's life is the person themselves and that no amount of experience or academic qualification can ever preclude the necessity to understand and work with the whole person. This highlights the most important quality of any therapist to be that of empathy, which is the ability to see and feel their client's world in something of the way they do. Without this skill every approach, whether psychological or spiritual, will simply result in telling people what to do. Such an attitude demonstrates great immaturity, is likely to prove a major set-back in the life of anyone who comes for counselling, and is the antithesis of good counselling.

Our supreme example of this principle is the person of Jesus. He surrendered His position with The Father in order to experience life on earth in the same way we do. This means that whenever we come to Him with our trials and tribulations we know that He really does understand us. No wonder He is called "Wonderful Counsellor" (Isaiah 9 v 6).

1

UNDERSTANDING THE TERMINOLOGY

There are a great many models of counselling and they utilise very different approaches to understanding the way people work. Even the approaches that claim to be Christian can vary enormously in their understanding and interpretation of The Bible. For some, The Bible is the only book required and everything else is seen as unnecessary and a distraction that will only serve to dilute the message. At the other end of the spectrum are those who believe, since the secular world has made such incredible advances in understanding the way human beings function, that we should be committed to embrace every bit of the latest psychological thinking. However, those who hold this view generally are not quite sure whether The Bible should be used in counselling at all.

> *"Some authors develop specific approaches to counselling calling their models 'Biblical' in some way. Some counsellors use The Bible simply as a reservoir of helpful material whereas others say they are Christian but do not use The Bible at all"* (Capps 1981 p12).

To be able to work as a Christian counsellor requires more than being a person who has trained to be a counsellor and who happens to be a Christian. It is also much more than someone who claims to be a Christian attempting to work as a counsellor. Although elements of the training and experience in each of these disciplines can be seen as absolutely essential, they don't combine automatically when trying to help someone deal with the problems and difficult issues in their life. There are many people who possess a great deal of knowledge and experience who have a genuine desire to be of significant help to others who are going through difficult times in their life, but their appreciation of what comprises a counselling relationship is severely lacking.

For the purposes of this book I want, first of all, to define what I mean when I refer to someone as a Christian. It is someone who has; acknowledged their own inherent sinfulness before God, accepted that Jesus died to pay in full the penalty for all their sin, confessed their sin to God and in an act of repentance been willing to turn and be different, invited Jesus to come into their life as Saviour and Lord, received the Holy Spirit of God to be their constant counsellor and guide, and made a commitment to study and live in obedience to the teachings of The Bible in all its fullness. This is meant to distinguish what I mean by a Christian from someone who simply 'goes to church' or has grown up in a Christian environment. A friend once told me that he was actually born in a fire station, but he quickly added "But that doesn't make me a fire engine!" It follows, therefore, that whenever I talk about a Christian, I am referring to a person who meets the above criteria as opposed to someone who may call themselves 'Christian' because they are connected to a local church. Therefore, those who may be offering counselling cannot be considered to be Christian counsellors just because they are operating under the auspices of a church or within a church setting.

Let us now consider what I mean when I use the word 'counselling'. There can be many variations of interpretation here, but there are several significant elements which are required to satisfy the definition. Here are several definitions written by counselling students on a degree level course:

> *Counselling is a formally agreed and completely confidential process where a qualified counsellor is accountable, through a recognised Code of Ethics, to an appropriately qualified counselling agency, team, or organisation and who is receiving regular and formal counselling supervision.*

> *Counselling is an activity which seeks to help people towards constructive change and growth in any, or every, aspect of their lives through a caring relationship, within agreed boundaries, and which is carried out by an appropriately qualified counsellor.*
>
> *Counselling is an arranged interaction between a qualified person (or counsellor), who puts no pressure or demands upon a recipient person (or client), in which the counsellor creates an environment where the client feels safe and comfortable to begin to accept responsibility for completely re-appraising their own situations and circumstances.*

Most attempts at defining a counselling relationship are usually aimed at helping people understand what they may be letting themselves in for prior to engaging in the activity for themselves. But any short definition of counselling is unlikely to adequately or accurately convey all the important aspects of the counselling relationship, which is why the Ethical Framework for the Counselling Professions, produced by the British Association for Counselling and Psychotherapy (BACP) is now more than 13 pages in length. The BACP is one of the leading accrediting bodies of counsellors in the UK, and here is one short definition they produced in 2013:

> *Counselling and Psychotherapy are umbrella terms that cover a wide range of talking therapies. They are delivered by trained practitioners who work with people over a short or long term to help them bring about effective change or enhance their well-being.*

The Association of Christian Counsellors (ACC) is, as the name suggests, an accrediting body for Christian counsellors and they produced a short definition of their own which was published in 2009:

> *Christian Counselling is that activity which seeks to help people towards constructive change and growth in any or every aspect of their lives through a caring relationship and*

within agreed boundaries, carried out by a counsellor who has a Christian worldview, values and assumptions.

Many individual counselling organisations and agencies have produced their own short definition and here is a statement that was prepared by a Christian team - The Action Community Counselling Team, based in Abergavenny, South Wales in 2015:

> We offer a safe and confidential place for people to explore ways of moving forward in their life without being criticised or judged. Our team of qualified counsellors use an accredited Christian psychological approach which is completely non-discriminatory and we are happy to work with anyone regardless of their faith, background or circumstances

A common thread running through all of these definitions is the requirement for the counsellor to be someone who is qualified to work in this way. Most people believe they are qualified to counsel people because of the experiences of life they have been through and it is quite common for someone who is seeking counselling to ask to speak to someone who has been through similar experiences to the ones for which they are seeking help. This can be a common intention with people who are ignorant regarding the true nature of counselling. In reality, it is actually quite unhelpful if the counsellor has been through very similar experiences to the ones for which his client is seeking help, because it can taint his understanding of the client's story and colour the way he works with that person. It will frequently increase the likelihood that the counsellor will fall into the temptation to give advice.

Whenever a person seeks out help from someone who has had similar experiences, the chances are they will hear about what that person did to deal with those issues and will not be challenged to discover their own inner resources that can help them find the most appropriate ways forward for themselves. If a person who is going through a divorce chooses to seek counselling with a friend who has been through their own divorce, it is extremely unlikely that he will learn to manage his circumstances better or get any personal help at all.

Counselling training courses teach people how to keep their own life story separate from the client's information and learn specifically: not to give advice, not to make suggestions, and not to speak about their own experiences. The ability to do this has been described a bit like this:

> "as a counsellor enters the counselling room, he puts his own stuff in a box and leaves it at the door. He then seeks to enter his client's world as best he can and stay with that throughout the counselling session. At the end of the session, he puts the client's stuff into a box, leaves it in the room, and picks up his own box as he leaves the room".

This is a vast over-simplification of the process, but it conveys some very important principles that people are taught in counselling courses. A key rationale behind this is that the majority of people are just not able to do this until they learn and practice the relevant techniques as part of counselling training. Students will also learn two really important elements that make counselling different from many other forms of help and support that may be on offer. These are;

a) the requirement to respect the autonomy of the client, in other words, we must allow them the right to make their own choices and constantly encourage them to do so rather than trying to influence them in any way.
b) the requirement for them to make their own discoveries about themselves and the world around them rather than being told what to believe and what to do.

Counselling should be a pre-arranged private meeting between two people in a confidential environment. It is important for the counsellor to create a place in which the other person can feel confident and safe to talk about their difficult personal issues. A person who wishes to receive counselling may often be referred to as a counsellee, or a patient, but for the purposes of this book we will refer to such a person as a client. This should not be taken to mean that they will necessarily have to pay for the services they receive but this is merely used as a descriptive term for anyone who asks to see a counsellor.

Having identified what I mean by the terms 'Christian' and 'counselling', I need now to identify what I mean when speaking about the 'spiritual element', or the 'spiritual realm' of a person. A dictionary definition of spiritual is 'that which relates to a person's beliefs'. A belief could be described as a Trust, or a Confidence in something or someone, or a Conviction or Principle about something that is accepted as true – sometimes without proof. At this point it is really important to recognise that, although what I mean by the spiritual is quite different from religion, for many people there will be a large area of overlap between the two. However people choose to view this, it is an essential aspect of each person's makeup which must not be overlooked as part of the counselling process.

> *"Spiritual and religious matters are therapeutically relevant, ethically appropriate and potentially significant topics for the practice of counselling in every setting. Counsellors must be prepared to deal with their client's issues regarding the human spirit. Religion and spirituality are an important part of the client's problems and can therefore also be a part of the client's solutions. Because spiritual and religious values play such a major part in human life, they should be viewed as a potential resource in therapy rather then something to be ignored"*

Dr Gerald Corey. Cited in Sherman J. (2009) "Spirituality in Counselling" (p521).

> *"The spiritual dimension refers to our relationship to the beliefs, ideals, values and principles that we live by. This is the dimension of our overall world-view and ideological perspective, which determines how we operate in the other dimensions and how we make sense of the world".* (van Deurzen 2002 p92)

The fact is that, whether people realise this or not, everyone has a spiritual dimension but it might actually represent different things to different people. It can relate to the practice of prayer, meditation and contemplation as a means of inner development and personal connection with a higher power, which could be divine, human, natural, or mystical. It can enable a person to access their deep inner thoughts and feelings in an attempt to bring a deeper sense of peace and meaning to them. Bill O'Hanlon, in his book, "Pathways to Spirituality" says that spirituality is whatever helps you feel connected to something that is bigger than yourself, and he outlines seven different pathways to spirituality:

1. *Connection to the Soul, or Deeper Self that is beyond the rational, logical or emotional. It can be achieved through deep contemplation or meditation, by concentrated self-reflection and/or journaling.*
2. *Connection to, or through, the body can occur through the medium of dance or physical activity that produces a state of effortless, unconscious self-awareness which enables a person to be lost in their personal sensual experience.*
3. *Connection to another being, is an intimate one-to-one relationship which allows a deep transcendent connection. This can sometimes occur with a favourite animal or a beloved pet.*
4. *Connection to Community, involves that strong sense of belonging which can be felt, such as with family, church group, sports team, or social group, and prompts the need to spend quality time together.*
5. *Connection through Nature, is about being able to gaze at, and appreciate the elements of natural beauty that are all around us. The impact of beautiful things can produce a deep sense of fulfilment.*
6. *Connection through Creativity, relates to the great sense of satisfaction and reward which comes from being a channel. Artists, painters, dancers, musicians, and so on will often comment on the effortless flow that occurs when they are lost in their art.*
7. *Connection to a Higher Power, is the understanding that there is a greater intelligence than ourselves at work in the world and that, in some way, we can draw upon these supernatural resources.*

(O'Hanlon 2006)

The spiritual element can also include other aspects such as Comprehension, Conscience, Insight, Intuition, Sensitivity, Discernment,

Motivation, Desire, and Passion. It relates directly to our Core Beliefs, Core Values and Core Drives.

(Paul Meier et al (1991) "Introduction to Psychology and Counselling")

There are a variety of other terms that have been used to describe the spiritual realm such as <u>Transpersonal</u> – which literally means 'beyond the personal/self'. Transpersonal psychology may also include links to mystical states of consciousness, mindfulness, meditative practices, and shamanic states. It has strong connections with the meditative traditions of Buddhism and Hinduism amongst others and is known to be strongly multicultural. Another term people may come across is <u>Psychosynthesis.</u> This was pioneered by Dr Robert Assagioli (1888 – 1974), an Italian psychiatrist, who studied under Sigmund Freud. It was a development that came out of Freud's theories of unconsciousness when he was looking at the impulses that drive people towards a more authentic experience of 'self' as part of a larger reality. It involves the restructuring of the self in the light of the wider human potential for healing and wholeness. Another term associated with the spiritual is <u>Metaphysical Psychotherapy</u> and this can be traced back to the writings of Aristotle (384-322BC). This is a philosophical approach which relates to the abstract qualities of existence. It literally means 'beyond the physical' and looks at how people perceive the nature of reality.

It is not unusual to discover that many counsellors and psychotherapists choose to ignore the spiritual realm, or simply fail to explore it appropriately, but this tells us something about their own issues rather than about any concern for their clients and identifies a major deficiency in their ability to work with 'the whole person'. I suspect that most counsellors who fall into this category will tend to avoid the spiritual realm because they automatically link it to religion, and then have a real fear that it will prompt their biases, deficiencies or preconceived ideas to come to the surface. If we are to work effectively with our clients, we must recognise that every person has a spiritual realm and, for most people, this should be treated quite differently from any religious connection.

People still possess spiritual resources even if they profess to have no obvious connection to religion and do not subscribe to any particular religious beliefs. Helping people talk about what it is that gives them strength in times of difficulty and what motivates them to go on when everything appears to be against them, can be a vital source of information for the counsellor. Beginning to understand where they find their resources of energy and encouragement, and how they access these, are essential areas for the counsellor to explore with every client. Even the NHS has, in recent years, changed its view in this respect and has now incorporated this statement into its NICE guidelines:

> *Spiritual Care is that care which recognises and responds to the needs of the human spirit when faced with trauma, ill health or sadness and can include: the need for meaning, for self-worth, for self-expression, for faith support, perhaps for rites of prayer or sacrament, or simply for a sensitive listener. Spiritual Care begins with encouraging human contact in compassionate relationship, and moves in whatever direction the need requires.*
> (National Institute for Health Care and Excellence)

Helping clients draw on their spiritual resources is now widely recognised within the counselling fraternity as something that can increase the likelihood of good therapeutic outcomes whether they are physical, mental or emotional. It is therefore essential for counsellors to adopt a completely unbiased approach (as they would for any other aspect of therapy) towards moving into discussions about their client's spiritual dimension. Spirituality plays a meaningful part in the life of a majority of clients, and so to leave this out of the therapeutic relationship would be as much a disservice as imposing it on them would be (O'Hanlon 2006).

> *In the late 1990's patients reported that a spiritual dimension to mental health care helped improve their self-esteem and confidence, giving them a morale-boosting sense of better control in their lives. They described improved relationships, not only with family members, friends, carers and other acquaintances, but also – importantly for some – with God. On the whole they were less confused, less fearful, less angry, less guilty and less ashamed. They were altogether more relaxed about life and some found a new sense of meaning*

> *which resulted in a peace of mind that enabled them to both endure and to seek solutions for problems not yet resolved.*
>
> Taken from a study by Mary Nathan, recorded in *The Psychology of Spirituality (2011)* by Larry Culliford.

If I now want to bring all the above elements together and try to identify what I mean by Christian Counselling, there are a few additional principles which need to be borne in mind. The first of these is that I believe the best solutions in the world are always those which are grounded solidly on the principles of The Bible. In every area of life – business, commerce, relationships, health, education, finance, and so on, the solutions which work best are the ones which conform to Biblical principles. How could it possibly be any other way? The manual for any item of equipment will always include the very best ways of looking after it, because it contains the recommendations written by its maker.

We need to come to an understanding therefore, that God does actually have a plan and purpose for every individual, with absolutely no exceptions, and that He really does know what is best for us. Unfortunately His view is not quite the same as ours because He is more concerned with 'who we are', than with 'what we can achieve'. This means it is the spiritual process of who we grow into as we travel through life that is more important than any earthly objectives we might have. We must conclude therefore that every single obstacle or problem we face has a purpose. That means even the most awful, destructive and painful situations have the potential to work together for our good when we respond with the right attitude. Sometimes we only develop the qualities and characteristics we really need when we come face to face with the most serious challenges.

Christian Counselling therefore, is not simply about helping people find ways of avoiding or minimising their painful symptoms, but about helping people discover the amazing benefits of living in a right relationship with God. It works on the basis that if we are properly balanced and complete on the inside, the part we are able to take control over, we will be fully equipped to manage whatever happens to us on the outside, the part generally we are completely unable to control. Our supreme example and pattern in this respect is the person of Jesus Christ. He was never stressed, anxious or rushed, yet He never missed an appointment and always had time to talk to people along the way. He had complete peace of mind during the mockery of His trial and throughout His horrendous death, yet had nothing but love for his persecutors. He experienced total security all His days because He knew where He had come from, who He was, what His purpose was in this life and where He was going. There can be no finer model for us to seek to emulate and so the fundamental role of the Christian Counsellor is to help people become more like the person of Jesus Christ.

2

PERSONAL REVELATIONS

I have been a professing Christian for over 60 years and throughout that time I have continually been amazed by how many people seem to go through life carrying a mixture of fears, phobias and other burdens, and are holding onto searching questions which never seem to get answered. These concerns actually came to a head for me back in the 1980's when I was working in the Alps as a ski instructor and Bible teacher with Oak Hall Holidays. At the time, I was living out two of the greatest passions of my life: serving God, and Skiing.

From a very young age I had recognised the incredible opportunities and challenges which frequently come to the surface when people are on holiday and away from their home environment. I have very fond memories as an 8 year old at our church summer camp, seeing how people's lives could be changed, fears could be overcome, and a new sense of excitement and enjoyment could be realised. Perhaps it's the change of scenery, or being in a more relaxed setting, or simply not having to fulfil the normal everyday tasks with which our lives have become so familiar, but in circumstances like this, I never cease to be amazed at how readily people are to ponder, reflect and talk about the issues which are bothering them the most. Of course, I recognise that holidays are supposed to be the times when we leave all such issues behind, but because we find ourselves in completely different surroundings and without all the usual pressures, these kinds of issues will frequently find their way to the surface. If this is true of holidays as a general principle, it certainly seems to be the case with ski holidays and even more so with holidays that have a specific Christian emphasis.

The lightning bolt of personal revelation I am referring to in this section occurred in the resort of Zell-am-Ziller in Austria while I was teaching a group of beginners the basic principles of how to ski. The group consisted of a mixture of males and females of various ages and levels of fitness but, as I understood it, all were active sports people who had never skied before. Over the first few days of working with them I began to be intrigued by the way each person faced and tackled the various challenges which were presented to them and how this caused a variety of other, more deeply hidden concerns to rise to the surface.

At this resort the best snow and the nicest ski slopes for beginners were to be found around the mid section of the mountain and it required an initial cable car ride to get there. This, for one or two people, generated some serious bouts of anxiety relating to getting into lifts of any sort and managing heights, even before we got anywhere near the snow. Then, getting used to wearing heavy ski boots and managing heavy skis was a major concern for several people in the group. Coping with the cold environment was very difficult for some, whilst learning to trust their equipment was a massive step for others. Mastering the basic body positions can appear quite unnatural to begin with and this was a real obstacle for a few in the group whereas for others the fear of allowing both feet to slide at the same time whilst trying to maintain balance and control, was exceptionally hard to overcome.

Overall, on our first few days together, practically everyone in my group was grappling with one issue or another, but the most remarkable thing for me at that time was that I began to notice that none of these difficulties had anything to do with the size, shape, age, sex, strength or physical ability of the individuals concerned. Although it is quite normal for people who are new to skiing to be struggling with issues like these, I realised that in every case it was the internal mindset of the person that was creating the problem and not the external or practical issues with which they were grappling. This dawned on me when I began to make comparisons between those in the group who were struggling with something and those in the group for whom that same issue was not a problem at all. I began to experiment by using different approaches with each person, especially with those who were experiencing a similar problem. I started asking people what they were telling themselves as they faced their particular challenge.

At first, people weren't aware they were saying anything to themselves, but as I persisted in my questioning, I discovered that on practically every occasion, when someone found something really difficult to master about skiing, it was because there were powerful unspoken thoughts running through their mind which counteracted, or neutralised, the instructions I was giving them.

Whenever possible I tried to continue this discussion in the evenings and around the meal tables so that on lots of occasions I was able to help people identify a fear, or a belief that was limiting their ability to move on with regard to that particular issue. Sometimes I was able to help people deal with these internal issues straight away, and this nearly always resulted in a significant leap forward in their skiing progress, but at other times it was just not the appropriate time or place for people to face their issues so we would agree to leave them where they were for the time being.

The realisation that something was going on for people beneath the surface began to challenge the way I was relating to each person as a ski instructor, and this eventually revolutionised the way I approached all my teaching and training from that time forward. Although I didn't realise it at that point, this was also to form a foundational principle in my ability to provide counselling to people in the years to come. The principle of what I had discovered in people who were learning to ski, I found to be a similar underlying stumbling block in the lives of many people who get stuck in the trials and tribulations of everyday life. What happens is something from their past experience, which has made a significant impact on them, is continuing to have a strong influence on the choices and decisions they want to make in the 'here and now'.

During my time as a Baptist Pastor, I came across exactly the same kinds of difficulties in people who were struggling, or were stuck in some way, in their relationship with God and in the progress of their Christian faith. In lots of cases I discovered that some important events from the past were continuing to greatly affect, and often inhibit, the things they wanted to do in the present. I quickly came to realise that many Christians have learned to accept their doubts and fears, and continue to live with them as if that were normal. They carry on through life without ever having their key worries and questions resolved. These, along with dysfunctional habits and behaviours that are learned at an early age, frequently cause people to 'plateau' in their Christian life. I was struck by this again recently, when doing some research for a series of booklets on helping people towards Spiritual Maturity. I discovered that many people can be sitting in church every week, listening to powerful teaching from The Bible, yet don't ever get their really important questions, doubts and fears answered. By default therefore, they are allowing these concerns to continue to exert a powerful influence over the choices they make in their everyday lives.

The second foundational spiritual principle which became really significant to me in the early days of being a ski instructor was the principle that we all have the ability to allow another person to undermine what we are being taught. This principle reared its head one day when I was teaching a group of 9 to 11 year old budding ski racers at the Hemel Hempstead artificial ski slope. I had set a course of slalom poles down the slope and had positioned myself at the top so as to give each person some specific pointers before they set off on their run. I remember explaining that, as a means of not getting into bad habits at this stage, I wanted them to concentrate more on their style and body positions throughout the run and not to focus on their speed. I had been pleased to notice that the parents of most of the youngsters had gathered at the bottom of the slope and were yelling encouragement to their offspring at regular intervals throughout the session, until it dawned on me that they were actually timing each of the runs and then challenging their children to beat their previous time. These parents had brought their children to a 'race training' session and were doing their very best to ensure that their own child produced the fastest possible time. Unfortunately they had no idea that what they were telling their children was actually interfering with the development of their racing technique. By encouraging them to focus on the wrong issues they were allowing the introduction of bad habits and poor technique. Such habits can quickly become deeply ingrained, become very difficult to eradicate at a later stage, and can severely restrict the development of their skiing ability. I needed to explain to them that they were inadvertently jeopardising the future of their children as potential ski racers.

My time as a ski instructor showed me that the majority of people who might consider themselves to be experienced skiers will have picked up a bad habit or two in the early days of learning to ski, and these have become extremely difficult to eliminate. The result is that these will generally cause them to stagnate in their technical development and to reach a plateau from which it is hard to progress to more advanced skiing levels. Whilst this doesn't prevent them from enjoying themselves on the snow, it does make their skiing more demanding than it need be and can inhibit their sense of freedom to face and conquer the more challenging ski runs. Such habits can become so deeply ingrained that people become used to them and can convince themselves that it is just the way they are and they don't want to change. People then often don't want to make the effort to improve because it will involve going back to the basics and might rob them of some of their enjoyment. It is clearly not very helpful to just go around pointing out to everyone their weaknesses and deficiencies, so for most people any improvement is only likely to happen when they decide for themselves that they want to get better and choose to make their skiing technique more efficient. Until they become sufficiently dissatisfied with their current situation and see the potential benefits as worthy of making the effort, they are likely to stay as they are.

The examples I have mentioned here bear a direct comparison with the way in which we develop and grow in the Christian faith. Firstly, people will only be able to progress and grow in spiritual maturity once they can see that it is possible to deal with every issue that creates a blockage to their spiritual development. Secondly, many people reach a plateau in their spiritual development because of the advice they have been given by other well-meaning believers instead of reading the Manual for Life – The Bible – for themselves. They may be put off by the effort that could be required to make a change but then fail to realise that God has promised to provide whatever resources they may need. All that is necessary is for us to provide the willingness to return to the basics so that we can build again on solid and secure foundations.

Of course, this is not merely a problem for Christians but it is a common issue for people of any faith or of none – "How can I make my life more efficient, achieve real satisfaction and fulfilment, and dull the emotional and physical pains of everyday life?" This is a human problem in which people can become so desperate to receive some kind of help that they are willing to turn to any form of distraction that might provide it. This is where counselling may come into its own. True counselling is a process of helping people come to terms with their world by discovering an accurate interpretation of life's events and circumstances, without being indoctrinated with anyone else's opinions or beliefs. For this to be effective, it must be a journey of personal exploration for each person and not one in which they are pressurised, preached at, controlled or manipulated in any way.

As a result of my experiences as a ski instructor, as a pastor and as a counsellor, my objective in this book is to establish a clear rationale for counselling in accordance with the principles demonstrated for us in The Bible whilst taking advantage of modern advances in psychological knowledge and understanding. I firmly believe that The Bible gives us the only accurate information (from the maker's perspective) about the source of mankind's problems and it sets out the most appropriate pathways for us to deal with these issues effectively. However I also believe that, because The Bible is not a scientific or psychological journal, we must continue to learn more about how human beings have been fashioned by our creator together with how He has designed us to function so we will be able to discover better ways of helping ourselves and others.

3

THE CHRISTIAN PREROGATIVE

As I progressed through the early days of my secular training towards becoming a qualified counsellor I can remember numerous occasions when I was struck by the great similarity that existed between the psychological principles I was learning and the Christian principles on which my life was founded. It wasn't until much later however, that I came to the considered opinion that everything that works in psychological therapy, only works when it is in line with the way God has designed us. One of the foundational principles of everyday life is that if you want to know how something works, your best option is to consult the one who made it, and/or, carefully follow the maker's instructions that are recorded in the Operations Manual.

The more I studied the Scriptures, the more I came to realise that God has given us a pattern of how to work with people in times of their distress. He demonstrates this by the ways in which He chooses to work with us and He has recorded these in great detail through the pages of His Operations Manual, The Bible. Before I get into the detail about this, it is important for us to consider how the words 'counsellor' and 'counselling' are defined, according to The Bible. The Biblical principle 'to take counsel' means to consult someone who is generally recognised as being more experienced, older and wiser, and one from whom you would expect to receive good advice. This meaning has been taken up by the legal profession so that the solicitors and barristers a person might consult for advice in everyday life are usually referred to in court as 'counsellors'. This is an example of where the Biblical words have been taken literally rather than interpreted more appropriately.

You see, God doesn't actually give us advice. Instead, He sets out the facts, the principles and the standards we need to follow if we are to get the best out of life, then He gives us an invitation to explore these, to prove them for ourselves and, if we so choose, to apply them in our own lives. In the same way, the manual for your new car doesn't give you advice, it sets out what you need to do to get the best performance from your vehicle and you choose to accept this, or ignore it at your peril. Only the maker knows the intricacy of its design and therefore can tell you what will produce the best results. You don't consider the manufacturer to be dogmatic or controlling if the manual says your car runs on diesel fuel, and therefore you would be really stupid if you decided to fill the tank with methylated spirit for example, just because it is cheaper or more accessible.

In spite of this, it is generally accepted that as soon as you experience any problem with your car like a light suddenly appearing on your dashboard, it is perfectly natural for you to consult the manual. In other words, you seek counsel from the manufacturer. This establishes one of the most important elements about true counselling, and one which distinguishes it from many other forms of help – it should be readily available, but only provided at the request of the one who needs the help. In this way there is no pressure or manipulation applied and the complete autonomy of the individual is always respected. In the case of the car manual, the facts may be recorded and set out well in advance and they are never forced upon the recipients but are available to be accessed whenever the needs arise.

It may be helpful initially, therefore, to view The Bible in the same way. God has set out His clear guidance about how we can get the very best out of this life but He does not force these things upon us in any way. He allows us to access them as and when we may choose, or even to ignore them altogether. However, there is one thing of which we can be absolutely certain, although we have the freedom to make our own choices, we have no freedom to determine the consequences of ignoring the signals.

According to our manual of life (The Bible) therefore, the responsibility for making the right choices in our lives clearly rests entirely upon our own shoulders. However, the most amazing thing about God is that although He has given us the freedom of choice, even when we choose to live according to His recommendations, He doesn't expect us to be able to do this entirely in our own strength. Once we commit our lives to Him, He actually provides for us everything we need to be able to navigate our way through the journey of this life and to live in accordance with His principles and standards (see 2 Peter 1 v 3). Furthermore, when we go on living in a right relationship with Him, we are able to receive everything He offers, all we have to do is to ask.

It will be helpful at this point, in order to begin to understand what I mean by the term 'Christian Counselling', to consider how God provides counsel for us. The Bible attributes the term 'counsellor' to each of the following: Father (Psalm 16 v 7), Son (Isaiah 9 v 6), Holy Spirit (John 14 v 16), and The Bible (Psalm 119 v 24). Therefore, if we are to understand Christian Counselling correctly, it is essential for us to understand and attempt to emulate the ways in which God relates to us, as recorded in The Bible.

Let's look at each of these in turn: firstly, **Father.** As Christians, we recognise God as our Father because He is the one who gave us life initially and the one who gives us new life when we trust Jesus as Lord and Saviour. He is the ultimate authority, the fount of all knowledge and the one, above all others, who loves us and cares for us every day of our lives. He knows us better than we know ourselves and looks on the inner workings of our heart rather than simply our outward appearance. He has a divine spiritual plan for the whole of creation and sees us as an intrinsic part of that plan. He is the only One therefore who is able to offer us true counsel that is completely in line with the way in which we have been designed. One aspect that comes through to us in Psalm 16 is that it reminds us when we open our lives to the supernatural power of God, He will help us make sense of what He has already revealed to us and we can draw strength from the fact that He is always available to provide support and encouragement. He is the perfect example of the counsellor everyone would like to have.

Now, let us consider **The Son.** Jesus is the One who took on our form by being born as a human and chose to grow up through childhood and adolescence by managing the physical and emotional trials of everyday life in our world. The record of His life gives us a clear demonstration of how to live victoriously in this world by facing every situation in the power of The Father's provision. Because He is God, He is constantly aware of the spiritual dimension in our lives and is uniquely positioned to identify with the stresses and strains we are facing. Therefore He is able to offer us true counsel that is perfectly in line with The Father's plans and consequently He is referred to in Isaiah 9 v 6 as 'Wonderful Counsellor'. Throughout His life we see that He does not tell people what to do and does not answer direct questions about Himself. Even in His 'Sermon on the Mount' (Matthew chapters 5, 6 and 7) He merely taught the principles and standards the Father had already laid down as a pattern for wholesome and successful living, but presented them in language that people could more easily understand. He never pushed himself forward or sought any glory or recognition for Himself instead; He wanted people to discover for themselves the reality of who He was. No wonder people flocked to Him in their droves and hung on His every word. He is a perfect example of the highest form of counselling.

Next, let us look at **The Holy Spirit.** He is the supernatural power of God whose specific tasks are to guide and prompt us into following God's plans and purposes and then to empower us to be able to carry them out. He is the perfect gentleman; He never forces us into anything but is constantly urging us to respond to His encouragement to become more like Jesus. He is not only around us wherever we may go, but comes to reside within us which gives Him a unique perspective on the way we are dealing with every issue in our life. In John 14 v16 Jesus portrays Him as the 'Paraklete' (Greek), or helper. He is the One who comes alongside us to bring comfort and encouragement, the One who opens our eyes to the truth of God's Word, the One who prompts us to respond to God's love, the One who reveals to us the reality of what we are really like on the inside, the One who motivates us and empowers us to boldly walk forward into God's specific purposes for our life. He never takes decisions for us, never barters with us, never seeks our approval, never accepts our excuses, and is never fooled by our inaccurate explanations. He is, in every way, the perfect counsellor.

Finally let us consider **The Bible.** It is the Word of God for every generation and is the final authority on everything to do with the Christian faith. It is our manual for life and it tells us about how God is working out His purposes for us as individuals as well as for the building and establishment of His Kingdom on the earth. It even tells us that *"All* *scripture is God-breathed and is useful for teaching, rebuking, correcting and training in righteousness so that the man of God may be thoroughly equipped for every good work"* (2 Timothy 3 v 16). It sets out the clear standards and principles that we were designed to live by, and gives us real-life examples of people who followed these, as well as some who didn't. In Psalm119 we see the writer referring to the value of meditating on the Scriptures in a way that allows them to become our counsellors (v24), that is, the words from which we can draw strength in times of crisis.

Reading, and applying, God's Word enables us to see ourselves more clearly, as we actually are in reality, rather than as we would like to see ourselves. It reminds us also that we have a blinkered view of life generally because we tend to see everything primarily from our own perspective, but there is a wider, more accurate view available to us if we are just willing to receive it. The Bible can never pressurise us or manipulate us in any way, but it can become a companion to bring light and hope into our lives in the very darkest of times. Hence, The Bible is the epitome of a perfect counsellor – it is available to turn to whenever needed, it reflects back exactly who we are, it cannot be phased by anything within us, it never changes with the circumstances, and it always holds out the hope of a better future.

Each of these examples demonstrate that our amazing triune God is the only person who possesses all these unique counselling characteristics and can understand exactly what is going on for us. He is the only person who can provide perfect counsel for us and so must be the standard by which we measure any human attempts at counselling. So if we take Him as our role model, we must also take on board <u>how</u> it is that He chooses to work. He never comes crashing into our lives to force His will upon us, He never puts us down, rejects us or ignores us. He hears every word we say and is constantly attentive to our real needs. He does not reveal our problems to other people, except in exceptional circumstances. He is totally consistent, righteous and reliable in every way. He respects us, loves us unconditionally, always sees the enormous potential we have, and always wants the very best for us. He gives us complete freedom of choice and even allows us to make our own mistakes without criticism or condemnation. He understands us even when we don't understand ourselves, He is able to see every situation from our perspective, yet is also able to see beyond this to where we have the potential to be. These, then, are the amazing qualities we aspire to in order to become effective Christian Counsellors, even though we recognise that because of our humanness we will never be able to fully achieve them.

Although I am quite clear about saying that counselling is a Christian prerogative, I am under no illusions that this gives us any right whatsoever to preach to clients. I believe adamantly that correct counselling protocol must be maintained in every counselling relationship at all times. There is absolutely no justification for a Christian counsellor to push forward their personal experiences, their faith, or their beliefs as part of a counselling session. Their role, out of respect for people's autonomy, is to help their clients explore for themselves every aspect of their psyche in a safe and unbiased fashion. So, whether their clients are Christian believers, unbelievers, people of other faiths, or of no faith, each person must be treated equitably and honourably and a trusting, proficient counselling relationship maintained at all times.

4

PERSON-CENTRED THERAPY

One of the most amazing developments in counselling and psychotherapy took place in the 1940's at the hands of an American psychologist - Carl Rogers. Up to that time therapy was generally conducted in a semi-dark room where the patient was lying on a couch with the therapist sitting out of sight at the person's head. The idea behind this was there should be no distractions as the therapist tried to get the patient to express their inner thoughts and feelings which were to be interpreted by the therapist. Carl Rogers came from a Christian background; his father was a Congregationalist, his mother a Baptist and his grandfather a gospel preacher. In his 20's he was considering whether to enter the full-time ministry but as a result of some serious doubts about his convictions he turned to psychology (Hough 1994). However, he never lost his willingness to acknowledge that people have a spiritual dimension and that this provides a significant key to understanding them. He later referred to this as 'mystical and transcendental' (Rogers 1961). It was his pioneering work with children that enabled him to develop the concept of a face-to-face relationship between a patient and their therapist, and that this had a much better chance of helping people deal with their problematic issues. In addition to this, his Christian background clearly seems to have influenced the development of his theories into what has now become commonly accepted as Person-Centred Therapy (Mearns and Thorne 1999).

It is generally recognised that there are three major 'umbrella' approaches in counselling psychology. These are known as; Psychodynamic, Humanistic, and Cognitive. Some other major headings have been recognised in more recent years but broadly speaking, all the hundreds of counselling approaches that exist, fall under one of these main headings. The therapeutic approach of Carl Rogers comes under the banner of humanist psychology which recognises that all human beings have an in-built capacity to grow towards achieving their full potential when the right conditions are present. For many years he worked alongside the psychologist Abraham Maslow who labelled this the 'Self Actualising Tendency'. They agreed that if the self actualising tendency could be harnessed, people could solve their own problems and heal their psychological hurts (Hough 1994). Consequently Rogers pioneered a non-directive approach to counselling in which he believed his role to be one where he would enable his clients to make their own choices in defining themselves rather than be pressured by the views of others.

As Carl Rogers was developing and refining his approaches to counselling he was not attempting to make any direct links with the Christian faith, and yet the majority of his foundational principles, in what he initially called Client-Centred Therapy, show a distinct resemblance to Christian principles. For example, he developed a series of his own principles for helping people that would demonstrate to them an attitude of Warmth and Genuineness. This aspect, for which he is most well known, is the identification of what he called his 'Core Conditions'. He maintained that when these conditions are correctly in place, they are totally sufficient to ensure that psychological growth and change would take place on the part of the client. His Core Conditions were:

1. Two people agree to be in <u>psychological contact</u>.
2. The first person, which he termed the Client, is in a state of <u>incongruence,</u> producing vulnerability and anxiety.
3. The second person, which he termed the Therapist, is <u>congruent</u> and integrated in the relationship.
4. The Therapist experiences <u>unconditional positive regard</u> for the Client.
5. The Therapist experiences an <u>empathic understanding</u> of the Client's internal frame of reference and endeavours to communicate this to the Client.
6. The communication of the Therapist's <u>empathic understanding and unconditional positive regard is to a minimal degree achieved.</u>

Rogers maintained that no other conditions are necessary. He stated in 1957, "If these conditions exist, and continue over a period of time, this is sufficient - the process of constructive personality change will follow", (*The Necessary and Sufficient Conditions of Therapeutic Personality Change*). He later reiterated these in more detail (Rogers 1967) after a further four years of study at the University of Wisconsin. Whilst there may be differences of interpretation, in recent years it has become common practice to refer to psychological therapy as counselling, and to the therapist as a counsellor. From here on, therefore, I will use the terms 'therapist', 'counsellor', and 'psychotherapist' interchangeably. Now in order to understand the great importance of Rogers' Core Conditions, I want to unpack each of them in a little more detail.

CORE CONDITION NO 1.

What does it mean for two people to 'agree to be in psychological contact'? This is to be understood to mean they are engaged in a counselling relationship. There are now much clearer guidelines and recommendations, produced for example by The British Association for Counselling and Psychotherapy (BACP), about how such a relationship should be established and that this should take the form of a structured agreement. Such standards did not exist in Rogers' day but are now seen as being essential for the understanding and protection of both Client and Counsellor. The main principle here is that the client should be seeking counselling of their own free will and the counsellor should be offering counselling having explained what it is and how it works. It should be explained that the relationship is intended to become a partnership in which each person plays an equal part on an equal footing. It is quite common, therefore, for client and counsellor to have an informal conversation about whether they are willing to work together in this way prior to the commencement of any counselling sessions, so that an agreement can be reached in this regard without coercion of any sort. Many counsellors though, may choose to include discussions about such a contract, (or working agreement), at some point during the first few counselling sessions with a client. Whatever approach is adopted here, it is important for both parties to be clear about what the relationship is going to entail, what boundaries need to be established, and how confidentiality is going to be maintained. No competent counsellor would consider offering counselling without putting such an agreement in place.

For the Christian Counsellor, the process of agreeing a formal contract at the start can be even more important. It will help to ensure any possible misunderstandings about the nature of the relationship can be avoided and help remove any doubts about the way confidentiality issues will be handled. Any thorough approach to counselling is going to involve a psychological and spiritual relationship of some depth and so a clear explanation of these points is essential prior to commencement. However, even when this is carried out, to establish this in an atmosphere of care and humility can be easily overlooked. Within the Christian church there can be many ways in which help and advice may be offered and this can be provided by a whole variety of different people who may or may not be qualified to do so. We will consider some of these in more detail in chapter 10. It is really important therefore for every person who would like to receive counselling to be crystal clear about exactly what is involved in the process they are about to begin. They need to be clear about what role the counsellor is to play and clear about the role they will be asked to play in order for the process to be successful.

CORE CONDITION NO. 2

In this Core Condition Rogers identifies the person who would like to receive counselling as 'the client'. Rogers describes this person as being 'in a state of incongruence which produces vulnerability and anxiety'. He maintained that incongruence can most easily be understood as a discrepancy between the person's real self (who they are) and their ideal self (who they wish to be) which will usually generate some unsatisfactory and inappropriate responses for the client. People therefore generally come to counselling because they have a concern with which they feel unable to cope. Although such issues may frequently be triggered by exterior circumstances, it is the internal feelings and responses of the client that make the situation unbearable and drive them, sometimes as a last resort, towards counselling.

The issue is no different for the Christian counsellor in that clients may realise something is not right for them but they are not necessarily aware of what it is. They can feel vulnerable and anxious whether they believe it to be a spiritual issue or not. It will frequently be something with which the client may have grappled for some time without any success and may have sought help from a variety of other sources.

CORE CONDITION NO. 3.

The second person in the relationship – the therapist (or counsellor) – must be someone who is 'congruent'. That means the counsellor must not be experiencing the same kind of discrepancies as the client. For this Core Condition to be effective, he must be able to be genuine and authentic at all times, even transparent in the relationship. He must be open, honest, straight and true in every way throughout the sessions without displaying any preconceptions or biases. That will usually mean that he has been able to face, and resolve, any personal areas of conflict or intolerance that may have arisen in the past. To be congruent also means the counsellor is able to be fully present with the client without allowing any personal issues to cloud his perceptions. He must be completely non-judgemental in all matters, and have no hidden agenda.

This can be quite a challenge for the Christian counsellor who may easily feel prompted with a desire to share his faith and point people towards the Christian principles he has learned from his own experience. Rogers believed it to be essential for the counsellor to adopt a naive stance and be completely non-directive with each client. In this strict definition of counselling, other forms of help which may include elements of advice, guidance, and the sharing of personal experiences, cannot be properly regarded as counselling. This is an area in which many counsellors who fail to resist these temptations can, unwittingly, jeopardise the sensitive relationship of self exploration and learning for their client.

The Biblical concept of seeking counsel from someone who is more experienced does not equate to asking for help merely from someone who has been through the same issues. It relates to approaching someone who is wiser and has the perceptions and the tools to help the person get to the source of their problem before beginning to address the issues.

CORE CONDITION NO. 4

In this Condition Rogers makes the assertion that the counsellor should experience 'unconditional positive regard' for the client. This involves the application of three distinct elements in the way the counsellor relates to his client. The first of these is that he must be able to engage with his client unconditionally, or without any preconceived thoughts, ideas or judgements. The second element is that he must be able to maintain a positive attitude towards his client at all times, and the third element is to be able to constantly hold his client in high regard. In these most challenging aspects of the relationship there is absolutely no room for any personal opinions, any attempts to impart a solution to the client, or any negative responses to the client's behaviour. These qualities must not just be understood but must be demonstrated by the counsellor in a way that will allow the client to feel accepted, appreciated, valued and respected. Rogers described this as a 'prizing' of his client, a kind of non-possessive love and it is this that will encourage the client to feel that he is in a safe enough place to begin to freely express and explore his own issues without being judged.

These qualities bear an incredible similarity to the way in which The Bible teaches us to relate to others, whether or not they have a Christian faith. Jesus made it clear that He did not come into the world to judge the world (John 12 v47), and He was perfectly happy to associate with all people regardless of their background, condition, or circumstances. The apostle John writes in his letters about the importance of loving others in the way God loves us and Paul continually urges believers to value and respect other people. The key principle here is that no-one is any better or any worse than anyone else, we have all been created in God's image and we have all failed to live by His standards so this is no place for pride to creep in. The counsellor must maintain an appropriate sense of equality whilst demonstrating unconditional positive regard at all times.

CORE CONDITION NO. 5

This is another element which is absolutely essential for effective counselling to take place – the counsellor should be able to experience an empathic understanding of the client's internal frame of reference. Empathy has been described like walking in someone else's shoes, but it is so much more than this. It is beginning to see the client's circumstances in something of the way he sees them, and beginning to feel something of how he feels about things. Empathy is about the counsellor's ability to put himself into the client's world without losing his own. This is such a significant element that I go so far as to say that true counselling does not even begin if, for whatever reason, the counsellor is unable to experience this element. Without this level of appreciation the counsellor is most likely to begin to make his own judgements about what the client needs and the only option open to him then is to resort to giving advice or sharing personal experiences. Furthermore, making an empathic connection should never be a one-off occurrence for the counsellor, but it must be a constant process of attempting to maintain an in-depth understanding and connection with what is going on for the client at every stage.

This is an area in which many Christians fail; we become too impatient to get to what we think are the solutions to a person's problems before we actually understand the real issues with which the person is struggling. This usually means that neither counsellor nor client is able to get to the source of the problem and then, by default, we can end up trying to help by using a comparatively superficial approach instead of tackling the real issue. It is also a common mistake to ask too many questions. People do this because they think it will show they are genuinely interested in the client, instead of encouraging them to express in their own words what they really need to say. Every time a counsellor asks his client "How does that make you feel?" he is demonstrating that he has no empathy.

Holding the silences can be a great way of building trust with a client and showing that we are interested in them as a person rather than just in their story. Asking questions will frequently lead the discussion away from what the person needs to disclose and every question we ask, however well meaning it may appear, always comes from our own agenda. This can easily be interpreted by the client as an unhelpful power imbalance, but furthermore, the client will invariably respond from their head-knowledge rather than from the heart. In order to avoid this, we need to learn how to use key listening skills which will help our clients unlock what may be difficult to share because it lies buried deeply beneath the surface. It is our empathic connection that will keep us in touch with the client's inner world and will demonstrate our genuine concern to help them find a way forward.

CORE CONDITION NO. 6

Rogers maintained that all five of the preceding Core Conditions would be useless unless the client was aware of them, so communicating these to the client, and noticing the client's acknowledgement of them, is of the utmost importance. This becomes a vital part of the therapeutic process because it begins to alter the client's perception of themselves and builds a stronger connection with the counsellor which, in turn, increases their confidence and willingness to face their difficult issues. He believed that the client will respond to these conditions only if a true counselling relationship exists in which all the Core Conditions are being met. Only then, would positive psychological progress automatically result.

The essential characteristic of this approach is based on the assumption that each person is intrinsically good and that everyone already possesses sufficient innate resources to be able to deal with whatever traumas, conflicts or dilemmas come across their path. Furthermore, it is maintained that everyone has an inner motivation towards 'self-actualisation', or achieving their full potential and it is this that makes utilising the Core Conditions all that is required for progress to be made. Creating such a place, where the client feels safe, cared for and understood is not only seen to be a necessary ingredient for a successful counselling relationship but it is one which epitomises the Christian ethic.

Rogers' Core Conditions are pretty much a reflection of how God relates to us: we choose whether to engage with Him, He is the wholly congruent One, we come to Him in an incongruent state, He demonstrates unconditional positive regard for us, He has an incredible empathic understanding of our situation, He communicates these conditions through His Word, The Bible, and we have the capacity to immediately begin to make progress. Even then, our progress in life is not meant to be solely our responsibility but a partnership in which God promises to walk with us every step of the way. Of course, one of the great differences here is that God also offers to provide all the resources we are likely to need as we continue our journey. I believe, therefore, that these conditions should form the basis of every counselling relationship regardless of which psychological or spiritual approach is being used. Rogers summed up his philosophy in this way, but it sounds very much like God saying these words:

> *"If I can create a relationship characterised on my part; by a genuineness and transparency, in which I am my real feelings; by a warm acceptance and prizing of the other person as a separate individual; by a sensitive ability to see his world and himself as he sees them; then the other person in the relationship: will experience and understand aspects of himself which previously he has repressed; will find himself becoming better integrated and more able to function effectively; will become more similar to the person he would like to be; will become more self directing and self confident; will become more of a person, more unique and more self expressive; will be more understanding and acceptant of others; will be able to cope with the problems of life more adequately and more comfortably"*
>
> ('*On Becoming a Person*' Rogers (1961) P.38)

BASIC LISTENING SKILLS

We now need to consider what specific skills will be required to be able to conduct a true counselling relationship by keeping the focus entirely on the client without becoming directive or controlling in any way. This means not giving advice, not sharing personal experiences, and not asking questions about the client's circumstances. It sounds fairly simple to be able to do this, but in reality it is extremely difficult. In fact, for some people, at least to begin with, it would appear to be totally impossible. We are just not used to conducting conversations in this way so these skills have to be learned, yet they are the very basic skills of good listening and can only be mastered with plenty of practice. They include: -

1. Attentiveness – maintaining appropriate eye contact and good concentration.
2. Minimal Encouragers – the occasional 'mm' and 'eh eh' without interrupting.
3. Reflecting – repeating exactly a word or phrase without interrupting the client's flow.
4. Paraphrasing – repeating information back to your client in your own words.
5. Clarifying – checking that you have heard something correctly.
6. Mirroring – using body language to convey your connection to your client.
7. Focusing – helping your client come back to the main point of what they are saying.
8. Summarising – summing up the main elements of what you have heard so far.
9. Empathising – seeing and feeling things from your client's point of view.

Once these skills have been mastered, I believe it is possible to learn how to use the art of questioning most effectively. Without learning these skills first, people will revert to using too many questions and often use them inappropriately. Each of these skills will encourage people to say what they need to say without the counsellor needing to make suggestions, guess, take over, lead them, or try to solve their problem. Every Christian, regardless of whether or not they aspire to be a counsellor, should endeavour to acquire these skills.

THE MODEL OF CLIENT CHANGE

The Person-Centred approach is recognised not just as a therapy, but as a way of being which facilitates self-growth in the lives of those with whom we have a counselling relationship. When we operate the Core Conditions we enable people to realise, and move towards achieving, their own potential. It gives credibility to the 'whole person' of the client rather than focusing on any individual aspect of their problem and it enables the 'whole person' of the counsellor to engage with the client. The humanistic approach to counselling recognises each person as a unique individual who has a positive core which is constantly striving to achieve 'self-actualisation', or real satisfaction and fulfilment. It acknowledges the client's autonomy in making their own choices but seeks to help each person make such choices in the light of an accurate awareness of their own internal dilemmas.

For each one of us, our self concept develops over time and is formed largely from the attitudes and behaviours that significant others express towards us. If we are continually surrounded by the negative and dysfunctional responses of the people we care about, we will learn to hide our true feelings and build strong psychological defences against the outside world. It is these defences which need to be exposed in order that the true self can be brought into our conscious awareness. Person-Centred therapy believes that as the counselling relationship develops, and the counsellor demonstrates genuineness, non-possessive warmth, unconditional acceptance, and accurate empathy, the client will become more aware of his own negative influences and will automatically move towards becoming more true and authentic in their relationship to self and others.

However, these principles need to be balanced by some sensitive and appropriate challenges from the counsellor in order to help clients avoid the tendency to stagnate by feeling satisfied with just being more self-aware of the situation as it is. Unfortunately becoming self-aware does not always mean that people will feel ready to move into their new way of being. They will often need encouragement to explore the potential benefits more comprehensively before they allow themselves to make the transition. Counsellors can be equally guilty in this respect by colluding with their clients in the 1960's mentality of – 'If it feels good, it must be alright' – so why change?

From a Christian perspective, we believe that operating in a Person-Centred way, yet ignoring the spiritual dimension, although clearly capable of producing some extremely helpful results, could actually give clients a false sense of their own security. This kind of belief in their self-sufficiency can be liable to deteriorate into frustration if they are not able to sustain the progress they have made. This, in turn, has the potential to make their difficulties appear worse than they were before. Vulnerable clients who experience deterioration in their issues after having made progress can then easily seek dependence on some other form of support or addiction.

Many people who have gone through a period of counselling have come to the conclusion that counselling does not work because they have been able to make little real progress or to maintain it. This is often the result of a failure to completely understanding the way counselling works. It is the counsellor's role to manage the process but the counsellor cannot be held responsible for the way their clients choose to respond. Never-the-less it is a poor reflection of the counsellor's ability to function effectively if any client believes they have been let down because they were unable to make or maintain progress in their own strength. Christian counsellors therefore, must learn how to appropriately introduce the spiritual realm into their work without sacrificing the Person-Centred principles because whenever a counsellor fails to do this it will increase the likelihood of this kind of negative outcome.

5

THE EXISTENTIAL APPROACH

A dictionary definition of Existentialism is "a philosophical movement stressing the personal experience and responsibility of the individual, who is seen as a free agent" (Collins 2009). One of the main things that differentiates Existential Psychotherapy from both Psychoanalytical therapy and the Cognitive and Behavioural therapies, is that it views life as a reality to be experienced instead of a problem to be solved (Tan 2011). From a Christian point of view, one aspect that helps to make this distinction is the priority that is given to the spiritual dimension. It is seen in Existentialism as an element that requires an equal amount of attention to the other elements of the psyche yet is one that is completely overlooked by many other psychological approaches. The Bible tells us that we have been created Body, Soul and Spirit, therefore any therapeutic process which ignores the spiritual dimension is, at best, only going to access two thirds of a person's problem. However, experience dictates that the majority of the problems which people bring to counselling are actually rooted in their spiritual dimension. This means that any approach with clients which ignores the spiritual dimension will simply not be likely to address any of the real issues.

The Existential philosophical approach to counselling is one which can generally be traced back to the Danish Christian theologian and philosopher Soren Kierkegaard (1813-1855). He is regarded by some as the father of existentialism, although Otto Rank (1884-1939) is considered to be the first Existential Therapist after breaking away from Freud in the 1920's. Rank was the first to view therapy as an experience of learning and unlearning. He maintained that it is the unique relationship a client forms with their therapist that allows them to learn ways in which they can let go of their self-destructive thinking and feeling in order to embrace their true self. He was a great pioneer in the field of Existential Psychotherapy and Transpersonal Psychology.

It was Jean-Paul Sartre (1905-1980) who is credited with developing specific elements of psychological exploration and was the first to use the term *existential*, but it was Rollo May (1909-1994) who continued to develop this approach into a more practical form of therapy. Later, Viktor Frankl (1905-1997), an Austrian psychoanalyst who was imprisoned in a Nazi concentration camp during the Second World War, identified from his experiences that if people have real purpose or meaning in their lives they are better able to face all kinds of negative and destructive circumstances which might otherwise be difficult to survive. He called his development of the existential therapy process 'Logotherapy'. Within it he highlighted the importance of the attribution of meaning to everything in life and claimed that everyone has an in-built drive towards realising this, but that this frequently gets buried under our efforts to become acceptable to the world around us.

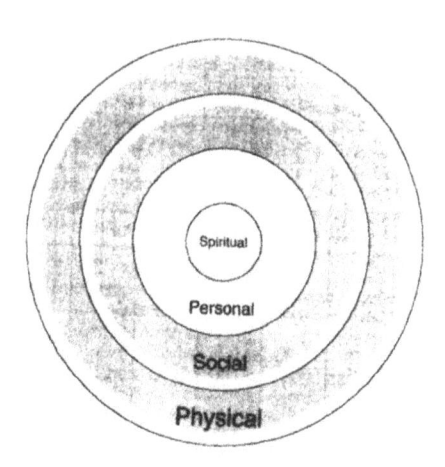

van Deurzen E and Adams M. *Skills in Existential Counselling and Psychotherapy, pp16.* Copyright c 2011 by Emmy van Deurzen and Martin Adams Reprinted by permission of SAGE Publications Ltd.

The Four Dimensions of Life

Emmy van Deurzen (born 1951 in The Netherlands) studied in France where she achieved a Masters Degree in Phenomenology and Existentialism, and later introduced the concept of four realms, or spheres, as a way of understanding how each person experiences the circumstances of their world. The four realms she identified are: the Physical or Biological (Umwelt), the Social or Relational (Mitwelt), the Personal or Psychological (Eigenwelt), and the Spiritual or Abstract (Uberwelt). In each of these realms there is a paradox to be faced and the extent to which people are able to acknowledge and handle these paradoxes is, she maintained, the extent to which their lives remain balanced.

She pioneered the principle of using Edmund Husserl's phenomenological method of enquiry (vanDeurzen 2011), to help clients unpack each of these areas and to bring them into their own conscious awareness. This requires the counsellor to develop some specific skills: a) to 'bracket' their own material, b) to get the client to describe in detail what is going on for them, c) to resist the temptation to put any personal emphasis or interpretation onto the client's information and d) to get the client to make their own choice about what is most important for them.

Irvin D. Yalom (born 1931 in Washington), is an American Existential Psychiatrist who has pioneered further developments in Existential Psychotherapy. He maintains that mental health problems are frequently caused by the way people battle with the vital issues of their existence; their fear of death, their drive towards freedom, their desire to avoid isolation, and their desperate struggle against the principle that everything in this life is meaningless. He calls these the four 'givens' of human existence and maintains that the quality of a person's life is determined by how they react to these.

He elaborates on what Existentialism is and demonstrates by his own practice just how important a role it can play in psychotherapy. He defines it as "a dynamic approach to therapy which focuses on concerns that are rooted in the individual's experience" (Yalom 1980, p5). Loosely put, he explained that Existentialism is simply about what exists, although he later introduced a much greater sense of structure to the existential approach. He shifted the counselling emphasis onto the counsellor's ability to appreciate how aware the client is of these key dilemmas of life, and stressed the importance of assisting each client to discover their own solutions. Respecting the client's autonomy has always been seen as a really important aspect of Existential therapy.

Existential therapy includes helping the client to see that what they are is a direct result of the choices they have made, in the light of the circumstances they have faced. To assist this process, the counsellor should endeavour to establish a strong empathic connection from the very first encounter and then seek to maintain this throughout each subsequent session. This allows for the use of the phenomenological method of enquiry (PME) to be most effective as the counsellor helps the client to accurately identify their responses along with any repeated patterns of responses in each of the realms of their story. Phenomenology literally means the study of events and things as they show themselves (van Deurzen 2011). A most important skill at this point is the counsellor's ability to sit with not knowing, that is, allowing the client to expose his own details at his own pace without interruption or judgement. This is only likely to be achieved through effective use of the basic skills of good listening, as identified in the Person-Centred approach (see page 33).

The Existential approach to counselling and psychotherapy is all about helping the client to identify and explore his own meanings and values so he can make informed decisions about what he wishes to keep, and then helping him to live authentically within these parameters. It also includes a recognition that we have all created our own identity up to now, and are continuing to do so with every decision we make. As psychotherapists we are not concerned with helping our clients to resolve their problems but instead helping them to acknowledge the inevitability of disruption in each of the spheres of their life, and to enable them to review the way in which they choose to handle these occurrences. It is helping them to come face to face with themselves, their values, assumptions and ideals in order to decide how they wish to move forward for the future.

> *I sometimes describe my role to people as being that of a 'psychological gardener', that is, I help people dig up, root out, and dispose of anything they consider to be harmful, dangerous or undesirable in their life so that, going forward, they can plan to plant, nurture and cultivate whatever they decide is healthy, wholesome and beautiful (Trevor Summerlin 2018).*

The Christian counsellor can learn much from the Existential approach by recognising that the issues with which each person struggles are rarely simple but can have implications and develop influences in other less obvious facets of their life. Many of the decisions and choices people make on a daily basis will be heavily influenced by their core values and beliefs so an exploration of these is extremely important.

A vital part of the process of being able to do this rests entirely on the counsellor's ability to enable the client to work through their four realms without feeling they are being interrogated but instead encouraging them to gradually bring each area into their conscious awareness. Whilst there is no specific formula for this, it can be helpful for the client to look at each of their realms in turn:

a) the physical or natural realm concerns the way they view their body, their health, and their abilities,
b) the social realm concerns the way in which they deal with their relationships and their intimacy issues,
c) the psychological or personal realm is where they identify and process their internal thoughts and feelings,
d) the spiritual realm is all about their core values, their inner resources and the meanings they give to things.

There is a sense in which the realms are interdependent, with each one having an influence on each of the others, so they may not appear as separate and distinct to a client when they are telling their story. The skill of the counsellor is usually required here to help the client appreciate the value of separating out their responses. It is most important that no aspect of this process should be forced upon the client, but the counsellor should be prompting a careful, thorough, and sensitive exploration of each area at the client's own pace.

During the process of exploring each of the realms, the counsellor seeks to draw the client's attention to how he is facing and managing each of the conditions of existence, or the ultimate concerns. These consist of four dilemmas, or paradoxes, and are sometimes referred to as the 'four givens'. The objective here is to bring into the client's awareness his attitudes, beliefs and feelings, and what he is doing to face and process each paradox:

a) <u>Freedom v Boundaries</u>, this relates to the ability to choose versus the need to conform, or our basic groundlessness versus our need for structure.
b) <u>Isolation v Connectedness</u>, is the awareness of our need to be separate versus our desire for connectedness, or independence versus belonging.
c) <u>Meaninglessness v Meaning</u>, in a world where there is no meaning we need to create meaning or, we believe there is no design and no purpose yet we are unable to live without them.
d) <u>Death v Life</u>, concerns the fear of death versus the fear of life, anxiety versus insouciance, or the inevitability of death versus the intense desire to live.

Through careful use of the Phenomenological Method of Enquiry the counsellor enables his client to reveal many of the underlying attitudes, values and beliefs from which his world has been created and is being maintained. From these revelations the counsellor assists the client to; identify his Sedimented Beliefs, understand his Locus of Evaluation, recognise his Conditions of Worth, notice his Patterns of Relating, and distinguish his Configurations of Self. The intention is that through this exercise the client will be able to view objectively, often for the first time, how his world is continuing to be constructed by his own responses.

His <u>Sedimented Beliefs</u> are those strongly held assumptions which he has allowed to settle in his psyche. They exert a controlling influence upon his day to day decisions and will usually have been generated either from his early life experiences or from powerful and significant life events. They can become so ingrained and habitual in the client's responses that it is possible to lose sight of, or even deny, their existence. In this case clients have often been known to comment "I can't help it, it's just the way I am". Identifying these beliefs and examining their source in order to re-evaluate them can only be done by the client when he is encouraged to bring them to the surface.

The Christian counsellor will require much patience and persistence to help the client identify his values and beliefs, because without doing this it will be extremely difficult to understand what is influencing his responses and behaviours. It will also make it unlikely for his client to make any significant progress in dealing with his real issues.

His <u>Locus of Evaluation</u> will be seriously dominated by the attitudes and beliefs of the significant people who have impacted his life in the past. The client's choices and evaluations in practically every respect will be dictated by what he believes would meet the approval of these influential people, regardless of whether their influence was for good or for bad. The way the client chooses to evaluate his own situations and circumstances is a conscious attempt to make himself acceptable to the outside world.

The Christian counsellor will recognise how common it is for people to behave in a manner they believe will give them a level of acceptability with the people they are trying to impress. This creates an unbalanced attitude which results in the development of inner conflicts and these will have a knock-on effect into every other area of functioning. The Bible says a double-minded person is unstable in everything they do (James 1 v 8).

His <u>Conditions of Worth</u> are, in a similar manner, those which have been foisted onto the client by other people who are generally in a position of responsibility or authority. A person who is continually hearing himself described with the same words time after time will eventually come to believe it for himself. It is then most likely that he will begin to behave in a way that is consistent with the words he is hearing, whether or not they are true. Where a client may be receiving conflicting conditions of worth, he is able to adapt his responses to suit the prevailing circumstances at the time as a way of trying to keep everyone happy.

For the Christian counsellor, we recognise that our sense of worth comes directly from God and not from what the people around us may think or say about us. Helping our clients to understand this can be difficult because many will not have the faith to accept this. So helping people to get in touch with who they really are is an important counselling skill which can open the pathway to areas of inner healing. This may involve getting the client to learn words of truth directly from the Scriptures.

His <u>Patterns of Relating</u> occur where the client is able to notice that his verbal and behavioural responses are beginning to be repetitive even when he is with quite different people and under completely different circumstances. This will often take the form of negative and inhibited responses but could equally be bold or extrovert behaviour. A person's external behaviours can always be seen as an indication of what is going on internally for him and can often reveal some quite deep issues. It can be quite easy for any of us to fall into adopting patterns of behaviour that have worked for us in the past and, even though our current circumstances may be quite different, we can find that we begin to rely on similar attitudes and responses.

The Christian counsellor should be quick to pick this up whenever this happens as the client is telling his story. People tend to rely on something they have used successfully before and this can quickly turn into a habit. Whilst there may be times when this can be really helpful, we are concerned to help the client deal with anything that stops him being authentic or prevents him seeing other possibilities in the way he relates to others.

His <u>Configurations within Self</u> refer to the different roles he is able to play without any apparent sense of conflict. He is able to portray himself as quite a different person in a variety of different situations by mentally separating out specific areas of his responsibility and involvement. Here it is possible for the client to see how contrary and inconsistent behaviours can be rationalised without realising they carry the potential for internal problems. It is possible for a person to convey the image of a controlling boss at work, the image of a loving husband at home, the image of a very efficient organiser in his social club, and a sensitive carer in his voluntary work at an old people's home. Whilst there may be no conflict between these roles, the counsellor is looking to see whether any of these are 'put on' to create a false image and whether any of these skills are transferable into his other roles. Where a client is behaving unnaturally, the struggle to keep each role completely separate from the others is going to create a huge amount of internal stress which will have a detrimental effect on his health and performance, both physically and mentally.

From a Christian point of view we can see how many of the above elements are often involved in the way people relate to God, to others and to themselves, and are the root of many stumbling blocks to their progress in the Christian faith. There can be no doubt that understanding these psychological and philosophical elements will be a most valuable help in enabling people to identify and remove any hindrances to their growth and maturity.

6

THE PSYCHODYNAMIC APPROACH

The term 'psychodynamic' refers to the transfer of *psychic or mental energy* between the different structures and levels of consciousness within people's minds and emphasises the significance of how the 'unconscious' continues to exert an influence onto the way people function (Nelson-Jones 2003 p3). The psychodynamic approach falls broadly into two categories: **Classical Psychoanalysis** which was developed by Sigmund Freud (1856 – 1939), an Austrian physician whose theory of the Psychosexual Stages of Development focuses primarily on a person's sexual development through childhood and adolescence, and **Analytical Therapy** which was pioneered by Carl Jung (1875 – 1961), a Swiss psychiatrist who broke away from Freud's approach to focus more on the life experiences of adults and their unconscious connections to the world around them. These concepts were later expanded by Erik Erikson with his Psychosocial Stages of Development where he maintained that people continue to face dilemmas at every stage of development throughout their whole life.

Freud introduced the idea that people have innate instincts which, when kept in balance, enable them to grow and mature in a healthy manner but which, when allowed to become unbalanced, will result in disturbed behaviour and significant problems in later life. He labelled these instincts: Eros or 'life force' which is our urge to survive, Libido or 'energy force' which includes our sex drive, and Thanatos or 'death wish' which relates to a love of danger or aggression. His theory is that if any of these were to become dominant in a person's life it would create serious problems for them. For example, a dominant Eros can produce all sorts of phobias and attitudes of selfishness, a controlling Libido reveals itself in an over-demanding nature, and an overpowering Thanatos will produce attitudes of recklessness, depression and suicide. Freud experimented with different ways to access these unconscious drives and frequently used 'word association' along with his interpretation of people's dreams as methods of doing this.

Freud then went on to identify three separate parts of the human personality and he maintained these also need to be kept in balance in order to avoid seriously disturbed behaviour. He called these: the Id or the 'pleasure principle' which we have from birth and demands immediate gratification, the Ego or the 'reality principle' which relates to our ability to learn to wait and develops in us at around two years of age, and the Super Ego or the 'morality principle' which we acquire at around three to four years of age and includes an ability to distinguish between right and wrong, sometimes called our conscience. Once again he maintained that if any of these become dominant this will manifest in disruptive behaviour: the Id will result in people wanting to live purely for their own pleasure, becoming hedonistic, wild and permissive, the Ego will produce people who are clinical, cold, and lack emotion, and the Super Ego pushes people into becoming moralistic, rigid, legalistic and unforgiving.

Whilst there are many things we can learn from Freud's deductions, the Christian understanding from the teachings of The Bible, is that we have been created in the image of God as tripartite beings, with a body a soul and a spirit, who have an intrinsic need to be in continuous relationship with our creator and with one another. It is generally understood that the human soul is made up of our mind, our will, and our emotions. It is also clear from the scriptures that we all have automatic drives and urges built into our human system, but Freud's assumption that these are all self-serving runs contrary to what The Bible describes as our need to be in a dependant relationship with our creator and the necessity we have to develop meaningful relationships with other people. Freud's approach to psychoanalysis treats any form of religious conviction merely as wishful thinking by putting the person as the centre and controller of life instead of

God. Classical psychoanalysis is essentially an agnostic or atheistic system (Jones and Butman 2011) which is primarily self-focused and self-serving.

Freud has probably become most well known for his psychosexual stages of development and, similarly, for his rationale that if people get stuck in any of these stages, which he called 'fixations', they will develop serious personality problems. He further maintained that if these remain unchallenged, they are likely to persist for the rest of the person's life. His stages of development are as follows:

1. The Oral stage (0 – 2 years) – this relates to babies learning to suck, bite, and taste when breast feeding. Therefore his Oral Fixations were as a result of babies receiving either too much or too little breast milk. Babies who receive too much breast milk, he maintained, become optimistic, selfish, lazy and expect everything to be provided for them, he called this 'Oral Optimism'. Babies who receive too little breast milk, he maintained, become negative, untrusting, doubting and cynical. He called this ' Oral Pessimism'

2. The Anal stage (2 – 3 years) – this relates to the child's ability to tense and relax the powerful sphincter muscles which Freud connected specifically to potty training. He claimed that children who were forced into this became 'Anal Retentive' with the attitude "It's mine and I'm keeping it". They were most likely to become mean, secretive, possessive, isolated, and obsessively orderly and tidy. Where potty training was neglected children became 'Anal Expulsive' with the attitude "It's mine and I want everyone to see". They were most likely to become extrovert, generous, gregarious, untidy and demanding of attention.

3. The Phallic stage (3 – 6 years) – this relates to the development of pleasure in the sexual organs. Freud linked this to the way a child forms an attachment to its same-sex parent and he claimed that problems in this area come from a poor Super Ego. Where a boy becomes over familiar with his mother and begins to be jealous of his father, he called this an Oedipus Complex, and where a girl becomes over familiar with her father and begins to be jealous of her mother, he called this an Electra Complex. The correct development of a close relationship will result in the

child adopting that parent's moral values or Super Ego and he maintained that failure to do this can produce homosexual and/or lesbian tendencies.
4. The Latency stage (6 – 11 years) – this relates to a period of high learning and skill development in which the child's sexual feelings are relegated to their subconscious until puberty. It is generally a period of great activity and creativity.
5. The Genital stage (12 18 years) – this relates to the time immediately after puberty when the child's sexual organs develop. At this time feelings for the opposite sex parent now begin to be projected onto appropriate members of the opposite sex.

Whenever a person gets stuck in any of these stages Freud believed they would immediately and unconsciously begin to develop their own mechanisms to hide this, so he treated all defence mechanisms as signals of underlying fixations. The fixations are never to be treated as the cause of the person's problems, but it will depend totally on the skill of the therapist to be able to interpret these signs so as to identify where the client's real problem is rooted.

From a Christian point of view, we may struggle to agree with Freud's methods of analysis, or with some of his conclusions, but we are compelled to agree that many behavioural traits which blight the lives of adults are likely to be rooted in their childhood and early life experiences. These will often have become such deeply ingrained habits that they appear to be automatic, even instinctive, patterns of responses. People who then learn to live with these can become convinced that they are unable to behave any differently. Perhaps one of the most significant things we can learn from Freud's work is that people's responses, whether verbal, emotional or behavioural, are never the real problem, they are but signals of deeper, underlying issues.

As Christian counsellors grow in experience, both in dealing with their own issues as well as through the experiences of working with their clients, it is possible to see how many of the difficulties that emerge in people's lives bear a striking resemblance to those Freud identified in his developmental stages. However, it is not necessary to accept the whole foundation of his psychoanalytical approach to be able to appreciate his contribution to understanding the source of our client's issues (Jones & Butman 2011). Nevertheless, we must be aware that Freud's original psychoanalytical approach completely ignores the Biblical principle that we have been created with an inherent need for relationship with God and with other people.

Freud used of the principle of free association, that is, he asked his clients to exercise a minimal level of conscious control whilst encouraging them to speak out whatever came into their minds as a means of revealing unconscious links to underlying conflicts or problems. This is something that is often referred to as a 'Freudian slip'. In a similar vein, he believed that the principle of transference which frequently occurs between a client and his therapist can reveal undisclosed 'fixations' with other important people in the life of the client. Christians are able to recognise that deeply buried negative opinions, beliefs and experiences can sometimes come to the surface at unexpected moments in the life of any believer. This was identified by the words of Jesus: "For out of the abundance of the heart, the mouth speaks" (Luke 6 v 45).

When Carl Jung broke away from Freud in 1913, he shifted the therapeutic emphasis away from a person's sexual development onto the development of a greater awareness of their own nature. He entitled his work **Analytical Psychology** and in this he stressed that a person's mental health was dependent upon unity and wholeness. He maintained that the personality, or 'psyche', was a combination of both conscious and unconscious thoughts, feelings and behaviours. He put a much greater emphasis on, what he called, the 'collective unconscious' which could be described as that which we have inherited from previous generations. He grew up as the son of a preacher and this may well have given him an interest in the spiritual dimension which he later developed to take account of the need people have to find meaning in life.

As Christians we believe that many character qualities and traits can be passed down to us from our predecessors but that not all of these will be positive influences. We may notice, in family photographs, a likeness that appears across several generations and we may recognise an aptitude to certain interests or activities that seems to be passed down the family line. The Bible teaches that it is possible for anyone to have some strong influences from the past which may continue to exert pressure on their present-day choices and, where these are negative, their hold needs to be broken.

Jung divided the human psyche into a series of archetypes, the major four of which he identified as follows: – The Persona which he described as a mask which we present to the world around us and which can vary according to our surroundings, The Shadow which consists of the repressed attitudes and desires which we keep hidden but which are prone to surface in our dreams, The Anima/Animus which is a combination of the male and female elements we each possess and which gives us a sense of wholeness, and The Self which represents the unification of our consciousness and unconsciousness by a process he called individuation. He acknowledged the importance of the fact that people go through various stages of development but, in contrast to Freud's work, he maintained that these were more to do with the social environment in which people grew up rather than their sexual development. This was later expanded more comprehensively by Erikson.

DEVELOPMENTAL PSYCHOLOGY

Erik Erikson (1902 – 1994) was a German Psychoanalyst who moved to America in the early 1930s. His work among children and young people provided him with the foundation to build upon Freud's stages of development and produce, with the help of his wife Joan, his own theory which he described as the 'Eight Ages of Man'. Erikson was the first major theorist to recognise the idea of life-long development. Through his 'psychosocial stages and tasks' he identified that at every stage of life people will face dilemmas and challenges and that these will continue to shape their character from birth to old age. He believed that at each stage people will develop simultaneously on three levels: biological, social and psychological and that each stage contains a paradox to be faced which will develop and reinforce particular character traits in each level. The following list of Erikson's developmental stages and the challenges to be faced at each stage has been adapted from the work of J. W. Van der Zanden (1977).

1. <u>Infancy</u> (0 – 2 years)   <u>Trust versus Mistrust</u>
   The child learns trust from the mother's attentiveness and reliability and perceives the world to be a place of safety in which to grow and to belong. Without this, the child will be likely to develop a sense of insecurity and vulnerability along with fears of rejection and abandonment.

2. <u>Early Childhood</u> (1 – 3 years)   <u>Autonomy versus Shame and Doubt</u>
   The child learns to explore and make choices which build a positive sense of independence. They gain confidence in their own abilities under the loving guidance of parental care. Shame and doubt develop from repeated failures and the condemnation of carers which can lead to obsessional qualities, being over-protective and critical.

3. <u>Childhood</u> (3 – 6 years)   <u>Initiative versus Guilt</u>
   The child learns to experiment with new mental and physical skills and abilities. Natural curiosity, the ability to play creatively and to fantasise should all be encouraged here. Where these are not tolerated the child's initiative is inhibited, closely followed by feelings of guilt for not conforming.

4. <u>Schoolage</u> (6 – 13 years)   <u>Industry versus Inferiority</u>
   Self esteem is a key element at this stage, including being valued by peers and adults. Personal beliefs, values, being competitive, and personal achievement are all essential here. Without achieving success of any sort the child will develop feelings of inferiority and become unwilling to try anything new.

5. <u>Adolescence</u> (12 – 18 years)   <u>Identity versus Role Confusion</u>
   Personal image is very important at this stage while rapid physical changes are taking place. There is a strong need to be accepted and to find a place in society. Sexual preferences may be explored as part of the struggle to become an adult. Conflicting responses from others and an inability to make personal decisions at this stage create role confusion.

6. <u>Adulthood</u> (18 – 40 years)   <u>Intimacy versus Isolation</u>
Developing close relationships to find a balance between giving and receiving is a challenge here. Striving for self fulfilment can produce fears about commitment and love, and being willing to lose personal identity in order to gain satisfaction can be frightening. Failure here produces feelings of insecurity and a tendency to withdraw.

7. <u>Late Adulthood</u> (40 – 65 years)   <u>Generativity versus Stagnation</u>
Being settled and mature at this stage allows for a change of focus onto external projects, family and community, with a willingness to pass on skills and experience to others. There can be a genuine enthusiasm and interest about life. Where earlier dilemmas and conflicts have not been resolved there is a risk of becoming stagnant, negative and inward looking.

8. <u>Old Age</u> (65 onwards)   <u>Integrity versus Despair</u>
This should be a time for demonstrating wisdom and of expressing satisfaction with the achievements of life. It's a time of reflection and recounting experiences as a means of encouraging others. Where negativity, bitterness and discontent prevail it is an indication that unresolved issues still lie beneath the surface and this destroys fulfilment.

As the principles of Developmental Psychology continue to be evaluated, many counsellors and psychotherapists believe that any of Erikson's original dilemmas can actually crop up at any stage of life and they are not exclusively linked to one particular age period. For example, the idea of developing 'Trust versus Mistrust' could occur for people of 65 years and over (Old Age) because of the environment in which they find themselves. Therefore, although Erikson's developmental stages can be a very useful guide, and may actually highlight the prime issue people face at each age, we must recognise that people will struggle with different issues according to the circumstances under which they exist. It seems quite clear that the way in which we manage every challenge in life has the potential to develop into a lifetime habitual response unless we take steps to avoid this happening or choose to resolve the issue once it has come to the surface.

Whatever difficulties a client may present to his therapist, it is essential for the therapist to create an environment in which the client feels safe enough to reveal and explore his issues with confidence and the most effective way of doing this is for the therapist to demonstrate Rogers' Core Conditions. Without these in place, there will always be a power imbalance between client and therapist and this has the potential to eventually sabotage the process. Many counsellors and psychotherapists who have not learned how to incorporate the Core Conditions seamlessly into their practice will struggle to create a trusting relationship with their client. This will frequently lead the client to believe they have not been properly understood and can produce feelings of disillusionment about the value of therapy. It is my considered opinion that every time a client says something like "Counselling didn't work for me", the counsellor must accept full responsibility for not establishing and maintaining an appropriate therapeutic relationship. The counsellor should try to ensure that every session develops a climate of trust, respects the client's autonomy, builds their confidence, encourages them to take appropriate action, helps them plan to move forward, and is a positive influence through times of doubt and fear.

The Christian counsellor must continually be aware that a person's responses, whether verbal, emotional or behavioural, are never the real problem but they will invariably be an external evidence of the way they have managed the earlier challenges and dilemmas at various stages of their life. It is also extremely likely that these signals will be strongly influenced by the person's values and beliefs and this creates a perfect opportunity to help the client explore their spiritual realm. Whilst later developments in the psychodynamic approach have appeared to be much more open to understanding the spiritual dimension, we must be aware that they are tolerant of all forms of spirituality, not just Christianity. However, that should not deter us from choosing to work in the realm of each client's understanding of spirituality. To avoid this is a dereliction of duty and increases the likelihood that the client will not face their real issues.

7

THE COGNITIVE BEHAVIOURAL APPROACH

The origins of behavioural psychotherapy can be traced back to early work on animal behaviour and learning, and among the earliest work in this field was undertaken by Ivan Pavlov (1849 – 1946) a Russian physiologist who is best known for his work with dogs which he called 'Classical Conditioning' (Feltham & Horton 2000). He noticed that dogs began to salivate whenever their food was being prepared and he called this an unconditioned response. Then he linked the presentation of their food to the sounding of a bell, and he noticed that they began to salivate whenever the bell was sounded even if no food was presented to them. He called this a conditioned response.

Work on continuing to observe how animal behaviour developed was conducted by B. F. Skinner (1904 – 1990), an American psychologist. He demonstrated that on the occasions when there was an increase or a decrease in certain behaviours, this could be linked to the event that immediately followed the first incidence of it and which served to reinforce the behaviour. If the event was a positive one it would increase the likelihood of the behaviour being repeated, so he labelled this 'positive reinforcement'. He also noticed that behaviours could be reinforced when they were followed by the absence of a negative event. He called this 'negative reinforcement' and labelled this whole aspect 'Operant Conditioning'.

The Bible gives us many examples of people who were conditioned by the environment in which they were brought up and demonstrates how challenging it is to even consider making a decision to change. However, it also shows quite clearly that it is possible for people to change if they are willing to exercise their God given ability to make their own choices (Joshua 24 v 15).

The actual practice of behavioural psychotherapy really began in 1958 with the work of Joseph Wolpe (1915 – 1997), a South African psychiatrist who refined his work whilst in the army dealing with 'war neurosis' – later to be known as PTSD. He worked on the principle that many of our behaviours are learned, and can therefore be unlearned. He developed a process of systematic desensitisation with people who were suffering acute anxiety and fear, and worked on 'assertiveness training' to strengthen their resolve and confidence.

Wolpe's work was, in many ways, superseded by the American psychologist and psychotherapist Albert Ellis (1913 – 2007). He originally worked alongside Freud but became dissatisfied with his psychoanalytical approach to therapy and pioneered the development of Rational Psychotherapy. This underwent a number of significant changes over several years as he continued to develop this approach. He began to get people to focus on their underlying, and often irrational beliefs, which he maintained were dictating their emotional and behavioural responses. He later entitled his approach Rational Emotive Therapy (RET) because he believed that irrational thoughts are the main cause of all types of emotional distress and behavioural disorders (Gross 1992). He deduced that irrational thinking produces an internal self-defeating dialogue which is made up of many negative self-statements and these in turn can manifest themselves in negative behaviours and phobias. He identified a series of basic irrational beliefs which he believed contributed to the most common psychological problems.

Albert Ellis began to use the following ABC system to help clients understand how they might differentiate between the internal source of their issues and the external symptoms, and then learn how to address these more appropriately:

A is the Activating event, the external circumstances, or the trigger.

B is the Belief clients hold internally about themselves and the circumstances.

C is the Consequential emotion they experience.

He used this as a means of helping people see that their problematic emotional and behavioural responses were not caused so much by the events they were caught up in, but by their own negative perceptions and self-beliefs. He also understood that negative behaviour can be generated both by negative beliefs as well as by negative emotions. To take this into account he later changed the title of his approach to Rational Emotive Behaviour Therapy (REBT) and was among the first to recognise the significant effect that people's internal thought processes were having in the determination of their behavioural responses. This eventually became widely accepted as the earliest beginnings of cognitive therapy.

"A strong empathic connection between the counsellor and his client will enable him to understand how each of these elements is contributing to his client's problems"

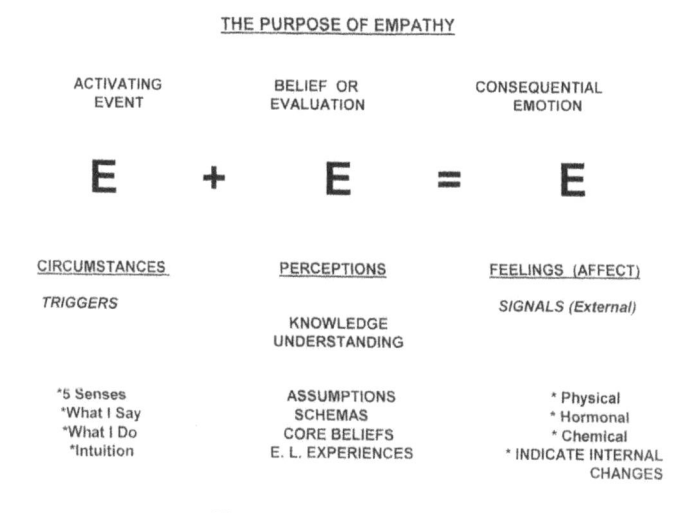

THE PURPOSE OF EMPATHY

ACTIVATING EVENT	BELIEF OR EVALUATION	CONSEQUENTIAL EMOTION
E +	**E** =	**E**
CIRCUMSTANCES	PERCEPTIONS	FEELINGS (AFFECT)
TRIGGERS		SIGNALS (External)
	KNOWLEDGE UNDERSTANDING	
*5 Senses	ASSUMPTIONS	* Physical
*What I Say	SCHEMAS	* Hormonal
*What I Do	CORE BELIEFS	* Chemical
*Intuition	E. L. EXPERIENCES	* INDICATE INTERNAL CHANGES

The Purpose of Empathy

The work of Albert Ellis had highlighted a most significant principle for psychotherapy, namely that the way people respond to their circumstances is not dependent upon their external environment but upon their internal beliefs. This highlights the foundational principle of the Christian gospel which is based on the intention that every person should be able to hear the good news so they are in a position to make their own decision going forward, regardless of their circumstances.

The most significant developments in cognitive therapy, however, came through Aaron T. Beck (1921 - 2002), an American psychiatrist, who is regarded as the father of Cognitive Behavioural Therapy (CBT). He was motivated by a quotation from Epictetus in AD 95, "Men are not moved by things, but the views they take of them" (Beck 1976). This formed the foundation for his development of CBT which went beyond the findings of Albert Ellis and could be summarised by the following rationale:

1. An individual's verbal, emotional and behavioural responses are determined by an immediately preceding cognition or thought.
2. An individual's cognitions or thoughts are constantly being influenced by their previously obtained knowledge and experience.
3. An individual's knowledge and experience is likely to contain distorted, maladaptive concepts as well as irrational and dysfunctional beliefs.

His strategy, therefore, was to develop a series of tools for the psychotherapist to use that would assist their clients in identifying, challenging and changing their negative concepts and beliefs. In this respect he was the architect of a process which encourages practitioners to pay much more attention to the cognitions, or thoughts, of their clients if they wish to help them create behaviour change and emotional well-being (Weishaar 1993).

Much of Beck's work was developed out of his approach to working with mental disorders such as anxiety and depression. He created a list of statements on which clients would give themselves a score at the start of each session to indicate the severity of the feelings they were experiencing at that moment. The Beck Anxiety Inventory (BAI) and the Beck Depression Inventory (BDI) enabled both him and his client to see specific evidence regarding any changes that were taking place. As a result of this, the importance of this aspect of his work became foundational to CBT. It was the first form of therapy to be evidence based and it relied heavily on the client and therapist working closely together, something he call 'Collaborative Empiricism'.

Beck went on to stress the importance of clients learning how to identify their own negative automatic thoughts (NATs), which were producing and maintaining their own dysfunctional behaviours, and then to set themselves goals for changing these. The process of change begins with the therapist teaching the client about the way the cognitive model works (Feltham & Horton 2000). Part of this process is to create together a 'Case Conceptualisation' which is a detailed outline of the client's issues and their possible sources, noting any repetitive patterns of negative thinking and behaviour. The conceptualisation, or formulation, usually begins by identifying a vicious spiral of current thoughts, feelings, actions, choices and beliefs, each of which is a contributory factor in maintaining the others, and goes on to include all the significant events and client responses throughout his life. This becomes an educational process, as counsellor and client collaborate together and it enables the client to identify and evaluate their own deep seated values and beliefs, whilst at the same time allowing the therapist to appreciate things from the client's perspective to a much greater extent.

A Cognitive Case Formulation

Triggers -   Events, Situations or Circumstances

Symptoms -

Feelings	(Emotional)
Sensations	(Physical)
Actions	(Behavioural)
Thoughts	(Rational)
Choices	(Volitional)
Physiology	(Biological)

Cognitions -   Negative Automatic Thoughts
(Linked to the Triggers)

Assumptions -   What I think is Fact

Critical Incidents -   These can happen at any age

Conditional Assumptions -   What someone has told me is Fact

Schema –   Maladaptive Coping Responses

Core Beliefs –   Deep-rooted Values

Early life experiences –   Mainly from 0 to 4 years

Birth –   Premature, Traumatic or Survival Issues

Pre-Birth -   Generational and Family Concerns

THE COGNITIVE CASE FORMULATION

An important Biblical principle here is that in order for people to develop and grow in their Christian faith it is necessary for them to learn how to identify and challenge every negative concept or belief they have and then to replace these with the truth as recorded in the Scriptures.

Beck believed that for CBT to be effective the greatest challenge for the therapist would be how to maintain a working relationship with each client that will encourage them to keep producing their own factual evidence. He therefore developed a range of skills, tools and strategies that would assist with this collaborative process. He believed that therapists need not only to be aware of such tools but must learn how to use them, must develop the skill to know which would be the most appropriate, and must learn when to introduce them so they could be most beneficial to the client. Some of these tools are as follows:

<u>Socratic Questioning</u> – a skilful form of dialogue in which the client is believed to already possess the answers to their own problems, so the therapist seeks to access these from the client's inner resources.

<u>Alternative Perspectives</u> – here the client is encouraged to think laterally and creatively, and to perceive his situation from different points of view.

<u>Forms and Record Sheets</u> – these allow the client to note the frequency and intensity of any problematic thoughts or other episodes. These can begin to show any patterns of responses and create visual evidence of the problem and its sources.

<u>Reality Testing</u> – this involves the client developing experiments that will enable him to examine what evidence there is to support or dispute a particular feeling or belief.

<u>Goal Setting</u> – the therapist should help his client set their own SMART goals (see page 119), then refine them and break them down into their smallest possible steps to increase the likelihood of successful progression.

<u>Homework</u> – what happens in between the therapy sessions can be a vital part of client progress so specific challenges for the client to work on can be agreed session by session.

<u>Schema Analysis</u> – this is an in-depth study of the client's subconscious attitudes and behaviours. It will often require the client to complete a detailed questionnaire followed by a careful and thorough investigation of the results.

Charts and Diagrams – there are a whole range of activities around the use of charts, diagrams and pictures which can be used to help clients accurately assess their current position and gauge possible outcomes prior to taking further action.

Cognitive Restructuring – here the client is asked to recall a particularly negative experience from their past and then encouraged to re-process the event to create a positive outcome in their mind.

Cost v Benefit Analysis – this process enables the client to make an assessment of what might be gained and what might be lost in relation to taking a particular course of action.

Challenging Beliefs – teaching the client how to identify their values and beliefs and then to question the relevance of them.

Gradual Exposure – the client is encouraged to face a particularly difficult issue in easy stages and in a controlled and supported manner so they learn how to control their own anxiety levels.

Relaxation Techniques – learning a range of skills and activities that can provide grounding and focus for the client so as to reduce anxiety and stress levels.

Unfortunately many people who have dabbled in cognitive therapy training, or taken a few weekend courses, are likely to have learned only a limited number of short term skills for client symptom relief. Furthermore they may have developed no real understanding of the CBT process, and may have no idea how to develop and sustain a strong empathic connection with their clients.

Whilst short term symptom relief may prove beneficial to clients, it can convey a completely inaccurate impression that cognitive therapy is simply 'a quick fix' solution. This is often borne out by many agencies who offer only a limited number of sessions to their clients which compels the therapist to focus predominantly on possible short term gains. Such an approach can damage the counselling relationship by creating frustration for clients when their symptoms return because they have not adequately addressed the source of their issues. An even more damaging situation however, is that without being aware of it, such an attitude can be doing a great deal of harm by undermining the image of the whole counselling profession.

A further problem exists for those who simply acquire a number of CBT tools which they plan to be able to use in an ad-hoc manner whenever the mood takes them. This approach lacks any consistency or continuity and can leave the therapist desperately searching for one gimmick after another (Freeman & Greenwood 1987). There really is no short cut to developing with each client a full and thorough Case Conceptualisation or detailed diagnosis. There is much evidence to support the fact that this will dramatically increase the likelihood of the client reaching successful outcomes in their therapy.

Some cognitive therapists find it really useful to help clients begin identifying their Schema (see appendix), which are the habitual attitudes and behaviours people use to cope with everyday circumstances and situations. Exploring these can be done concurrently with the production of the Case Conceptualisation so that each activity can provide insight and information for the other. The pioneering work on Schemata was conducted by Jeffrey Young who identified sixteen different, potentially habitual, negative and destructive responses which frequently emerge when people are feeling stressed. He also drew up a lengthy questionnaire which was aimed at helping clients recognise the ones they tend to adopt most frequently (Young & Klosko 1994). Working on this can prove to be a powerful and very revealing exercise and it can produce more practical evidence for the client of his most prominent attitudes, beliefs and most frequent responses.

For the Christian counsellor it is essential to appreciate the importance of the links between a person's thoughts and their behaviours; "For as he thinks in his heart, so is he" (Proverbs 23 v 7 New American Standard Bible), and to access their underlying motivations. It is also important to use appropriate skills that will help clients gain self-awareness at this level. On many occasions when church leaders have placed too much emphasis on the need for people to modify their behaviour they have missed the opportunity to encourage them to address both the root causes of such behaviour and the thought processes which are being used to sustain them.

By choosing to ignore the psychological principles of human behaviour in this way they are likely to increase the levels of frustration for the people concerned and this is likely to result in little or no significant change taking place.

The Bible does make it clear that what is stored in the hidden depths of our psyche will continue to dominate our thoughts and consequently provide a heavy influence onto many of our behaviours. 1 Chronicles chapter 28 verse 9 tells us that God understands every motive behind our thoughts, and Jesus explained to His disciples that negative (evil) thoughts actually come from the condition of our heart, or inner being (Matthew 15 v 19). Even the Apostle Paul was inspired to write that it is only a man's spirit that can know a man's thoughts (1 Corinthians 2 v 11) and it is the cravings of our sinful nature that produce the deep desires and thoughts within us (Ephesians 2 v 3). From passages like this we begin to understand how important it is for counsellors to take their clients into the spiritual realm so they might be able to access the potential source(s) of their problems.

8

MOTIVATIONAL INTERVIEWING

Practically everybody, at some stage in their life, would like to change something. Many adopt the idea of making New Year resolutions in order to be different in some way. Others may buy the latest self-help book, enrol on a course, start going to the gym, begin a new diet, take up a sport, hobby or activity, or even agree to see a therapist. Whatever our need may be, we all seem to struggle with the application of making a change, so counselling can be a good way to move forward because all good counsellors will work on the things their clients want to change. What we are concerned with here is not just the idea of doing something differently, but of changing our attitude to something that will enable us to grow and develop in a better, stronger, more beneficial way. For centuries people have been caught in the kind of dilemma where they desperately want to be different, and try really hard to be different, but end up falling back into doing the very thing they are trying not to do. The apostle Paul wrote, "I do not understand what I do, for what I want to do, I do not do, but what I hate, I do" (Romans 7 v 15).

Motivational Interviewing was developed by William Miller and Stephen Rollnick in the 1980s, building on the work of James Prochaska and Carlo DiClemente (1982). They had developed a model of how change occurs (Miller & Rollnick 1991) and had identified a number of stages that people pass through on the way to making an effective change. Although their work was intended initially to be a way of working with people who were caught in an addiction to smoking, they recognised that these stages could apply to anyone who is seeking to deal with any habitual problem.

Using this model they showed that each stage in the process could be used as a constructive part of a therapeutic relationship.

The Prochaska and DiClemente model consists of six stages, which allows the therapist to discuss the levels of internal motivation that his client possesses at each stage. It is a cyclical model and they found it was perfectly normal for people to go round all the stages several times before finally resolving the issue and/or settling on a stable change. One of the revolutionary aspects of this approach is that it recognises 'relapse' as being normal and it shows how this can become of significant benefit to the overall process. It is not meant to encourage people to relapse but rather to be a realistic element that will help to keep people from becoming disheartened, demoralised, or bogged down when a relapse occurs (Miller & Rollnick 1991).

The whole model is a process of helping clients clarify their own levels of motivation to achieve change and to recognise that they are already in possession of many of the factors that can provide an answer to their problem. It also works on the principle that people control their own willingness to change their behaviour but that this is only likely to be effective when they are ready to take responsibility for this. Change is not likely to be effective when people are told, urged or pushed to do so, in fact this is very likely to produce increased levels of resistance and a justification for keeping the status quo.

An oversimplification of the Motivational Interviewing process is that the therapist strives to create nothing for the client to push against, but instead allows complete freedom of choice at every stage and draws on the client's own rational ability. It is particularly useful with people who are opposed to change or are ambivalent about changing. The counsellor's role is to create an atmosphere that is conducive to change in which his goal is to increase the client's intrinsic motivation so that change arises from within rather than being imposed from without. When this approach is carried out properly, it is the client who presents the argument for change rather than the therapist (Miller and Rollnick 1991 p52).

Stages of Change Model

```
            1.
        PRE-CONTEMPLATION
                                            2.
                                    CONTEMPLATION
RELAPSE
  6.
              5.
          MAINTENANCE
                  Victory
                  Circle      DETERMINATION  3.
          ACTION
            4.
```

Adapted from Prochaska & DiClemente (1986)
"Towards a Comprehensive Model of Change"

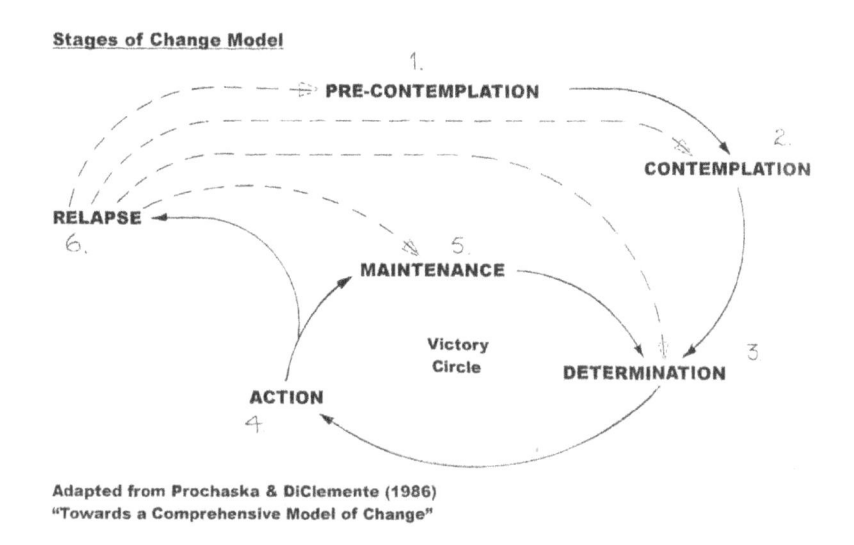

THE STAGES OF CHANGE MODEL

The Stages of Change Model gives the counsellor a practical framework that can be used with his clients to help them see where they are in their own process of effecting change. They are then able to work together to assess what is needed in order to move on to the next stage. In this way the client is not being judged but makes his own assessments and the role of the therapist becomes that of an informed assistant, encourager, supporter and guide.

STAGE 1 PRE-CONTEMPLATION

This is the point at which the individual concerned just cannot see there is a problem even though it may be blatantly obvious to other people. I regularly come across this situation when I am approached by someone who is concerned about another member of their family in the hope of getting them to attend counselling. It often occurs when a client is worried because they think their partner or a member of their family needs counselling. The person concerned may be in denial, be afraid, or simply be avoiding the issue. In the strictest of terms this is not counselling, but it involves providing detailed information in a way that will help the person who has the problem to see there are advantages in being willing to consider making a change. Great sensitivity is required to avoid the person being put off counselling completely, but the objective here is to create doubt in their mind about continuing as they are. It is about trying to increase the person's awareness of the risks and dangers of their current behaviour and helping them realise that alternative benefits and advantages are not only possible but desirable. Pressure of any sort at this point will usually sabotage the process completely so patience is essential.

A similar situation to this could arise whilst working with an existing client where a personal issue comes to the surface that has not previously been discussed and which the client expresses no wish to change. In this case it can be slightly easier to manage because a relationship of trust has already been established but it is still possible for them to be blind and in denial. The same levels of care must be exercised here if they are to be helped to recognise the problem for what it is.

A comparison can be made here with the vast numbers of the public at large who do not see any need to believe in God and are quite content to go through life in their own self-sufficient way. Many actually see Christianity as just another man-made religious crutch for weak people to lean on. Such people are unlikely to be persuaded or cajoled into changing their mind and can appear totally closed in their thinking about these things. A radical shift is only likely to be possible when they have a personal revelation, and a personal revelation is only likely to occur when they make a personal discovery. This means that our main objective should not be to convince them of the error of their ways, but to awaken within them a powerful sense of curiosity that they simply cannot resist.

At the pre-contemplation stage the Christian counsellor must resist any temptation either to point out the problem or to over-simplify the solution. A common mistake here is to read verses from The Bible which make it clear that the issue is not an acceptable one, instead of using counselling skills to help the client discover the problem for themselves. An even more damaging course of action would be for the counsellor to tell his client what the problem is, then seek to justify his actions by quoting references from The Bible that support this view. This must be a time of personal discovery and enlightenment for the client where any attempts to shortcut the process are most likely to have exactly the opposite effect.

STAGE 2 CONTEMPLATION

At this stage the client has now begun to think about the possibility that there just might be a problem, but they are not yet convinced about it and certainly not ready to address it. They need to be allowed to develop their own cause for concern but in the meantime be encouraged to express their ambivalent feelings openly. The counsellor must show a genuine interest in the reasons why the client does not want to change and be aware of all the advantages the client sees in making this choice. It is essential to resist the temptation to argue against these views and instead stay with the client's opinions. To allow the client to explain his views in great detail and to listen intently to them will create a strong empathic connection at this stage which will be most valuable as the process continues. It is sometimes hard to respect the client's autonomy when they appear to hesitate over making the kind of decision we want them to make and instead seem to settle for staying where they are now, but this is often a process of allowing the light to dawn slowly. Unless the client comes to his own decision about being willing to consider a change, the whole exercise will prove to be futile.

The Bible maintains that it is possible to reason this out logically. "Come now, let's reason together" says the Lord (Isaiah 1 v18), because it actually makes sense. At this stage we should be encouraging people to ask as many questions as they can think of and then provide them with all the support they need to help them explore and discover the answers for themselves.

The Christian counsellor must be careful not rush through this stage with his clients and understand that the responsibility for people to be convicted of the need for change does not rest with the counsellor, but with The Holy Spirit. Time should be taken to use additional counselling tools such as The Decision Balance Sheet (see appendix) which can be really helpful here. This can encourage detailed discussions about the advantages and disadvantages of making a change and can bring hidden desires to the surface for the client. We must be careful to accept our clients as they are now rather than have any preconceived ideas about what they might be like once a change has been made. Our unconditional acceptance of them is a pre-requisite for the work to begin and it is this that will facilitate change.

STAGE 3 DETERMINATION

This is the point where the client moves from a position of thinking about the problem to the point where he has made a decision to do something about it. This is really the point at which the therapeutic process is able to begin. Once a conscious decision has been made and there is a clear resolve to tackle the issue, the counsellor will work with his client to explore his levels of determination and commitment and his motivation to change. It will be reliant upon the client's understanding and appreciation of the benefits he will receive from making the change and this will only be enhanced when he can see the comparative disadvantages of staying where he is and resolves to be different.

The principle that counsellors must keep in mind at this point is that unless the advantages of making a change outweigh the advantages of staying where he is, the client is not going to make the effort to see it through. Competent counselling skills will be needed here to draw from the client a clear indication of his intent and to be satisfied that all his reasons for not changing have been countered. Time should be taken to use additional counselling tools and assessment sheets such as The Force Field Analysis (see appendix) that can prove extremely valuable during this stage. The skill of motivation is not telling someone what they should be doing, but it is tapping into something that already exists within the person. It must be this alone which creates the internal resolve for the client.

Many years ago when I was part of a sales team, our sales manager was trying to motivate each of us to increase our sales by offering what he thought would be an irresistible incentive – one week's all expenses paid holiday in Majorca. The guy sitting to the right of me immediately responded by saying "That's a complete waste of time for me because I own a time-share apartment and spend 3 weeks there every year". It was simply not an incentive for him at all, whereas the guy who was sitting to the left of me, who had never been to Majorca, thought it was a fantastic offer and was prepared to pull out all the stops to win the prize.

It is important to remember that because motivation is an internal thing any external pressure which is applied to people at this point is likely to produce the opposite result to the one intended. People must be determined to exercise their own will in line with the Biblical principle of personal accountability.

Christian counsellors should work with their client's core values to help create a discrepancy between the client's current behaviour patterns and how they would like to be in the future. Creating this kind of dissatisfaction without any pressure will encourage them to dispute their own behaviours and be the author of their own transition. It actively involves the client in developing their own problem solving skills which will also build strength and resilience in them for the future.

STAGE 4 ACTION

In this stage the counsellor is working with his client regarding the choosing and pursuing of a specific strategy. To do this effectively, and to avoid any sense of the client being persuaded or manipulated, it will require him to perceive a range of possible options. These need to be drawn from the things that are really important to the client, in other words, his values and beliefs. Spending time to get a client to talk about his core values can seem like unnecessarily going off at a tangent but, if his action plan is to work, it must be linked firmly to his own deep values and beliefs.

The process of identifying goals, making them SMART (see page 119), and then breaking them down into their smallest constituent parts can also be very time consuming, but the counsellor must realise how essential this phase is. If the client makes his goals either too easy, or too demanding, he will quickly lose interest and set himself up for disillusionment and failure. Often the initial goals the client chooses will need to be modified and updated several times as the process progresses. The objective here is for both counsellor and client to be satisfied that they have a workable plan to which the client is willing to be fully committed.

When attempting to cross a river, if the stepping stones are too far apart it makes the task too difficult and reduces the likelihood of success. Once extra stones are put in place, the chances of success are dramatically increased and it is easier for the person to measure his progress during the period of transition.

People who try to take massive steps or make dramatic changes in one all-or-nothing attempt are living dangerously and increasing the likelihood of getting it all wrong. Even when success is achieved, gains that are quickly made can be lost again equally quickly. Going through the process is part of the personal building and strengthening work that will help to sustain any progress made. In a similar manner, the Christian life is not a sprint but a marathon. Every challenge and obstacle presents us with an opportunity to grow, develop and mature so that we are better equipped for the future.

Christian Counsellors sometimes fail to realise the necessity of getting clients to establish their own goals during this stage, instead, preferring to press the importance of selecting goals based purely on Bible verses. The real skill in this phase is actually helping clients identify their values and beliefs according to Biblical principles. When this has been achieved, the goals will automatically become more appropriate.

STAGE 5 MAINTENANCE

In this stage the counsellor should help his client understand the need to build a robust supporting network and explore together how to put this in place. This can be a vital element in helping the client remain positive and stay on track. He needs it to provide constant and helpful reminders of the benefits, advantages, and the whole reason he is following this programme. It can consist of significant people as well as mechanisms, materials and activities that will help him persevere and keep focus in times of doubt or fatigue. He will be able to use these sources of encouragement to keep his motivation alive and tackle any obstacles or negative influences that may emerge along the way.

Times of difficulty can arise for everyone, sometimes without warning and often unexpectedly, but the most successful way of not being sidetracked by these comes from being prepared in advance. Becoming familiar with the people and the systems that the client can turn to in any emergency will be vital help-lines that can enable him to stay on track. This is not to be simply a list of friends, but of people who will be understanding and supportive of the client and who won't be fazed by any setbacks he may be experiencing.

The counsellor can be of most help here by asking his client to draw up a list of specific areas which could be problematic in the future and then planning together what action would be most effective to counteract each particular threat. There are all kinds of counselling tools and activities that could be of benefit here but a thorough approach to this is most important and it requires the client to be blatantly open and honest.

When the client is a Christian he could have a significant advantage here because he may be able to access a number of support services through his local church. There may well be people who have worked with others in similar situations and who can understand the necessity of this role. He will also be able to call out to God in prayer and use the resources of The Bible. The Christian Counsellor should spend some time helping his client create a list of appropriate Bible verses in a format that is easy to use, and not assume his client will know how to do this. Choosing to be involved in a range of activities or volunteering to help with charity work can also prove to be a great asset because it can provide the client with a completely different focus.

STAGE 6. RELAPSE

One surprising element of the Motivational Interviewing programme is that relapse is not only treated as a normal occurrence, but it is seen as a really important part of learning to build resilience. Relapse, or falling back into the bad habit, should always be treated as a positive, not because people should be encouraged to fail, but because people should be taught how to learn from the experience. Even a tiny lapse, or a temporary slip, can be the first step on a slippery slope into relapse and should be treated seriously. Every lapse is an opportunity for the counsellor to work with his client to analyse exactly what went wrong. Every step should be re-traced to discover the point at which the slip began so the client can create his own corrective measures and immediately put these in place for his own future protection.

In the case of the man who got drunk after being sober for some weeks: it wasn't trying to be his old self with his mates that did it, it wasn't being persuaded to go for 'just one drink for old-time's sake' that did it, it wasn't going past the pub where he knew his mates always hang out, it wasn't walking down the street where his favourite pub was located, it wasn't deciding to go for a walk hoping to bump into some old mates, it wasn't even the gut wrenching feeling of missing his drink. No, it all started when a drink advert came on television and he couldn't look away. Holding this picture in his mind allowed it to fester beneath the surface until he contrived an innocent plan to go for a walk. Once he had established the point at which the whole process was triggered, he was able to resolve to immediately look the other way every time any advertisement for drink appeared. He then chose one of his support team to whom he would make himself accountable in this respect on a regular basis.

I have a friend who has not taken an alcoholic drink for over 30 years but he still chooses to cross the road so as never to walk past the door of a public house because he doesn't even want to pick up the smell. The counsellor must get his client to identify every tiny area of weakness in dealing with each particular issue so his client can decide on what action to take if ever it should arise. Alan Marlatt identified 5 Steps which will take a person into Lapse, each one leading to a situation more serious than the one before:

1. An apparently irrelevant decision leads to -
2. A high risk situation which leads to -
3. A no-coping response and an inability to resist which creates -
4. A feeling of helplessness, shame and lack of control which leads to -
5. A positive expectancy of feeling better and being accepted.

Once a lapse has occurred there is an increased possibility of it occurring again so Marlatt went on to identify a further four steps which he said will generally lead from Lapse into Relapse:

1. Stress – because the person has broken their own rules
2. Self-Blame – beating themselves up because of their weakness
3. Using the Habit itself to reduce stress and guilt by feeling better
4. Using the good feelings to justify the need to continue

(Marlatt & Gordon 1985)

When a lapse or a relapse has occurred, if the client so desires, it is possible to return to any of the other stages of the process. However, the counsellor should help his client to question very carefully which would be the most appropriate stage at which to recommence work on the process again. Clients who choose to dip in and out of the process because they are convinced they can easily start again are unlikely to achieve any levels of long term success.

Within Christian circles, relapse is generally not looked upon very favourably and is often treated as failure. The Christian counsellor will need to examine his own understanding of this if he is to be effective in this area. The fact is that anyone who wants to learn a new skill must be prepared to make mistakes and to learn from them. People who have grappled with issues in this way will invariably end up much stronger than those who experienced an easy ride and never had to struggle to achieve. The Christian counsellor should appreciate that we have all fallen in some way and failed to live up to God's standards so he does not emphasise the guilt aspect to his client. Instead, he must choose to focus on the lessons that his client can learn as he looks for, and analyses, new ways to become stronger.

To experience consistent victory over his problem the client must plan to stay in the 'victory circle'. It is the act of repeatedly going through these three stages that will develop an inner strength. Each time the client is in the Maintenance stage he should begin to look for another facet of his problem to challenge and then move on to the Determination stage again before putting it into practice in the Action stage. In this way he will be able to keep his focus on moving forward and resist any temptations to lapse.

9

VARIOUS CHRISTIAN APPROACHES TO COUNSELLING

My very first connection with counselling came as a teenager when I volunteered to help lead people to Christ at the end of a Billy Graham rally which was being screened in our local cinema. After Rev Graham had delivered his message, he always asked people to respond by coming forward to the front of the auditorium. I was then allocated to someone of similar age and my role was simply to take them through a series of steps explaining the gospel, and then encourage them to pray a prayer of life-changing commitment by accepting Jesus as their Lord and Saviour. I was part of a large team of people who in that context were known as 'counsellors'. I believe, because this initiative which Billy Graham used was so successful, it has coloured the understanding of many people since that time in terms of what is involved in Christian counselling. The result of this is that the majority of church people tend to treat the role of a counsellor as someone who gives directions to people and tells them what they should do. Many non-church people have also developed the false assumption that anyone who is linked to Christian counselling is only going to want to preach to them or try to persuade them into the Christian faith.

Depending upon who you speak to about Christian counselling, it can be taken to mean anything from secular psychology practised by someone who is a Christian, or Biblical counselling practised by someone who is completely opposed to all psychological insights (Anderson 2000), to a professionally qualified counsellor who is able to thoroughly integrate sound psychological practice with profound spiritual insight. Counselling approaches that are merely linked to Christianity can vary from, what Selwyn Hughes described as, 'The Christianised Counsellor' or someone who uses Bible language but has no experience of a personal relationship with Jesus to, what I call, 'The Religious Counsellor' or someone who simply quotes Bible verses to people and sends them away to sort their life out. I am appalled at these extreme approaches and I do not recognise them as acceptable counselling approaches, in fact I even question whether they can be Christian and whether there is any evidence of the qualities of Jesus in these approaches.

Although we may recognise the deep significance of the spiritual dimension, we must also consider the attitude of some people towards the integration of psychological principles into the realm of Christian counselling. There is a strong feeling in some quarters that using anything other than the text of The Bible to minister to people's needs is simply unacceptable, and literally unbiblical. The theory here is that The Bible is the all-sufficient Word of God and therefore absolutely nothing else is required to be able to minister to people, regardless of what their needs might be. One argument used regarding this form of Christian ministry is that to draw upon resources other than The Bible is like admitting The Word of God is inadequate for every task. Some have even gone so far as to say that anything that is not received by direct revelation from God must be treated as satanic.

My definition of a Christian counsellor therefore, is someone who is able to combine sound Biblical teaching with sound psychological principles into the practice of effective psychotherapy. Later, we will look in more detail at a specific model which seeks to embrace each of these elements. That is not to say people cannot be helped by experiencing these weaker approaches but, since my whole focus in this book is about becoming a Christian counsellor, I want to draw attention to some of the most prominent practices that have come under the 'Christian' umbrella and review some of the advantages and disadvantages of each.

~ Trevor R. Summerlin ~

CHRISTIANISED COUNSELLING

This term can be used about any form of counselling that gives an impression of being Christian without having any significant Christian foundation. There are people who think if they use a form of therapy that has a link to some aspect of Christianity they will either gain a higher level of respectability for themselves and their practice, or people will simply take more notice of what they are saying. This can include people who consider themselves to be 'church' people because they are regular attendees of a local church, or because they want to work with clients who have church connections, or even because they are in a leadership position in the church. The Christianised approach can also include any form of counselling that may be carried out within a church building or by any ordinary church member.

Whatever the motivation of the helper might be, it is important to recognise that there is no magical benefit from making this kind of connection. People who use this kind of approach have been known to use Christian terminology, or Bible language and may refer to Christian standards of living as a way of trying to get their clients to adopt what they are saying, but this usually boils down to their desire to give advice and direction rather than to use genuine counselling skills.

For a counsellor to be sympathetic to Christian principles does not make it appropriate for them to use this as a means of coercing their client into making progress. Even in such cases where the person is a qualified counsellor, to exploit this kind of connection to Christianity is really a misrepresentation of their role. Of course, it may not always be done deliberately or in a preconceived manner. It is possible for a counsellor to drift into doing this as part of an attempt to try to be helpful to a client, but this is a bit like trying to make use of an aspect of psychological theory without understanding how it fits together in the wider picture of human behaviour and will, as a result, tend to convey a completely inaccurate impression of the abilities and motives of the counsellor.

All counsellors should, at any point, be able to give a detailed explanation of the approaches they use, how they fit together, and how they are relevant to the process in which the client is engaged at that time. All clients who are receiving any form of counselling or psychotherapy should not hesitate to ask questions of their counsellor about anything that is being said to them, or about any aspect of the counselling they are receiving. The whole process is so much more effective when the client is able to fully appreciate what the counsellor is asking of them and how it can contribute to their development and learning. The counselling process should never be secretive in any way but be an open exploration of the client's issues with client and counsellor working in partnership together. I encourage people to be very suspicious of any counsellor who is unable or unwilling to provide thorough, in-depth answers to any questions they may be asked regarding the techniques they are using.

NOUTHETIC COUNSELLING

This approach to Christian counselling was pioneered by Jay E. Adams in the late 1960s and outlined in depth in his book "Competent to Counsel" (Adams 1970). It is a confrontational and challenging approach which is based on his understanding of passages from The Bible which seem to urge Christian disciples to adopt what is almost an aggressive approach to sharing their faith. He goes to some lengths to define what he describes as 'nouthetic confrontation', and includes words such as 'warn', 'teach, and 'admonish'. He says that it comes from the Greek word *nouthesis,* which conveys the idea that something in a person's life needs to be changed in order for the person to conform to Biblical standards of behaviour. He is not concerned to discover why people respond in the way they do, but is interested purely in what they need to do to make the necessary changes (Adams 1970 Ch 4).

One element about this approach which causes some concern is that the teachings of The Bible indicate that any time we wish to administer words of correction to others this should be carried out in an atmosphere of love and care for their well-being. However, the very nature of Nouthetic Counselling appears to make it essential for counsellors to become more confrontational than is really necessary. Although this approach is firmly rooted in the authority of The Bible, it encourages counsellors to quote Scripture and speak to people in a challenging and confrontational manner without demonstrating a high degree of love and care. It identifies that all sin, or the failure to live according to God's standards, creates a blockage in our ability to live a godly life and will therefore result in problems and difficulties coming to the surface. "Thus the goal of nouthetic counselling is set forth plainly in the Scriptures: to bring men into loving conformity to the law of God" (Adams 1970 p55).

The Nouthetic counsellor will expect clients to take responsibility for their failures in this respect by admitting their guilt, confessing their sin, and seeking forgiveness in Christ, but this can easily be interpreted as a judgemental, almost condemnatory attitude. To believe that The Bible contains all the answers for every one of life's difficulties is actually an over-emphasis of the role of Scripture. Whilst The Bible does set out God's standards and principles for living a successful and satisfying life in harmony with Him, and it identifies specific rewards and advantages attached to this, it does not explain exactly what we need to do in every situation in order to achieve this.

The Nouthetic counselling approach relies heavily on the interpretations of the therapist and does not seem to convey the patience and sensitivity that is often required to walk alongside a person who is grappling with the difficulties of living a practical Christian life. This suggests two specific problems for the counsellor: 1) to home-in on a client's problem without developing a clear understanding of how the client sees his problem will always result in the counsellor putting his own interpretations and solutions onto the issue, and 2) to confront the client's issues by helping them get right with God without helping them build spiritual strength and resilience for the future is going to appear judgemental, critical and uncaring. Furthermore it can significantly increase the pressure on a person at a time which is already stressful for them. Such attitudes will only serve to create an appearance of superiority and prevent the formation of any real counselling relationship. It also tends to remove the elements of personal discovery and achievement which are vital for real character change and growth to take place.

Jay Adams was very critical of anything to do with encouraging people to focus on their own self-image. He used words like "pagan" and "a plague" to describe the self-esteem movement. He argues that The Bible does not intend to make us satisfied with ourselves, or self-sufficient in any way, because that will only lead to self-worship. Instead we are to maintain a focus on self-denial and the constant recognition of our human sinfulness (Collins 1989).

I believe that counselling, in the truest sense of the word, must be a partnership between client and counsellor where the counsellor is using appropriate skills to enable the client to make his own discoveries about the source(s) of his issues and then plan his own pathway for moving forward. In Christian counselling, this principle becomes even more significant because we should be aiming to deal with people in the way God deals with us. Those who fall into the trap of trying to help their clients by giving directions, making suggestions, giving advice, or talking about their own experiences under similar circumstances, are simply demonstrating they are not competent counsellors.

PASTORAL COUNSELLING

Almost at the other end of the counselling spectrum from the Nouthetic approach is the Pastoral counselling approach. The term 'pastoral' comes from a Greek word which relates primarily to the work of shepherds in finding good pasture, taking care of, and protecting their flock. In The Bible, the role of a shepherd is likened to the work of a church leader and many non-conformist Christian church leaders take the title of, and are frequently referred to, as Pastor. It generally carries the connotation of humbly helping to meet the needs of people in a way that will enable them to grow and mature in the Christian faith. The apostle Paul puts it like this in The Bible:

> "Be like-minded, having the same love, being one in spirit and purpose. Do nothing out of selfish ambition or vain conceit, but in humility consider others better than yourselves. Each of you should look not only to your own interests but also to the interests of others. Your attitude should be the same as that of Christ Jesus". (Philippians 2 v 2- 5)

Pastoral counselling therefore, is really a composite term which conveys both the aspect of helping people deal with problems in their life, as well as helping them get their needs met. Since this frequently involves a practical activity on the part of the helper, it probably should be referred to more accurately as Pastoral Care. Historically, four different aspects of Pastoral Care have been identified and these are described as 'sustaining', 'reconciling', 'healing' and 'guiding' (Clebsh & Jaekle 1964). Although there may be both similarities and differences in these elements, the predominant factors in each of them are friendship and providing help. This is borne out by Roger Hurding's description of pastoral counselling as a process of making friends with a person in order to offer advice (Hurding 1982). There are a great many people who are desperate for friendship and this can quite clearly be a source of comfort and healing but should not be confused with the development of a more formal counselling relationship.

Evelyn Peterson maintains that genuine caring will always lead to counselling (Peterson 1980), but for counselling to be effective clients must be able to make a clear distinction between the two. It is my considered opinion that when a person is going through a period of counselling they are likely to need the support and encouragement of friends around them, especially if they are facing difficult emotional issues. For this reason people should never consider offering counselling to their friends because this will only serve to undermine the high standards of the counselling profession by creating confusion over issues such as boundaries and confidentiality, and can rob people of important shoulders to lean on when going through times of crisis.

Pastoral care can be conducted in a much more fluid, relaxed and sometimes spontaneous fashion whereas counselling should be conducted in specifically arranged appointments within a confidential environment. Notwithstanding this, Pastoral counselling is now increasingly being offered by non-church organisations such as in industry, commerce and education where Chaplains and/or Human Resources personnel are being appointed for this task. We must therefore understand the difference between someone who is using counselling skills as part of their normal job, and someone who is a qualified counsellor who chooses to conform to a specific code of ethics (Lyall 1985). It is now quite common for pastoral counselling to be offered in a whole variety of situations without reference to anything Christian but it is also quite common for many churches to be offering pastoral counselling without any understanding that the people who are offering this should be properly trained, should have appropriate qualifications, and should choose to make themselves accountable.

BIBLICAL COUNSELLING

As we have already identified, not all approaches to counselling that are called 'Christian' will be solidly based on the teachings of The Bible, and even those which claim to be so based can vary greatly in their interpretation and application of Biblical teaching. In the late 1960s Dr Larry Crabb, an American Clinical Psychologist, utilised his knowledge of secular psychology to identify both its strengths and its weaknesses when he considered various theories alongside the teachings of The Bible. He maintained that "the obvious need in the field of counselling is a clearly stated unity within which there is room for diversity" (Crabb 1989 p25). By first establishing from The Bible a solid foundation for understanding human problems, he was then able to draw upon some of the developments of secular psychology to build a process that he maintained would help people tackle their issues effectively. He called his approach Biblical Counselling and it was substantially different from the Nouthetic approach of Jay Adams who rejected everything that was not included in the Biblical text.

People who adopt Adams' approach and insist that secular psychology has nothing to offer are labelled by Crabb as 'nothing butterists' – nothing but The Word, nothing but The Lord and nothing but their faith. Crabb is equally scathing about those therapists who choose to take bits of The Bible and try to make them fit with bits of psychology. He calls this 'the tossed salad approach'. Similarly, I have come across a great many 'counsellors' who say they adopt an 'eclectic' approach by which they mean they use a whole variety of different psychological approaches depending upon what they think will be most beneficial to their clients - and this will always be according to their own judgement at the time. Whenever I have spoken to people who adopt this approach, I am struck by the fact that they have a little knowledge and understanding about a lot of psychological principles but with no real depth of understanding. Consequently they are often unable to demonstrate any real ability regarding how best to use their techniques to handle difficult client issues.

Whether they include any Christian aspects, or not, this 'pick and mix' approach can cause great confusion for a client because as soon as a difficulty arises in the use of one particular approach, the counsellor is liable to hop to a different one. Such a lack of consistency makes it very difficult to follow anything through to a conclusion and can give the impression of a distinct lack of structure. The result of this is that counsellor and client rarely seem to know where they are in the process. "Without the solid foundation of a true, unchanging understanding of man and his problems, eclecticism can become a technical disguise for sloppiness and guesswork" (Crabb 1989 p25).

Crabb was adamant that Christians must be free to profit from the thinking of secular psychologists but must carefully screen and reject any concepts which contradict Scripture (Crabb, cited in Benner 1987). Biblical counselling must therefore be founded on the infallible Word of God and help people to discover that there is a plan and a purpose for their life which is available only through a personal relationship with Jesus Christ. Crabb identified two key elements which underlie the issues with which most people struggle: a) they have a desperate need for significance, and b) they have a desperate need for security, so he developed a model for counselling that would enable his clients to specifically address these needs. The model was a seven stage programme with each stage being a pre-requisite for the next. He would take his clients through this systematically using a variety of psychological skills at each stage. His model was as follows:

1. Identify the client's negative feelings,
2. Identify the client's negative behaviours,
3. Identify the client's wrong thinking,
4. Teach the client right thinking,
5. Secure the client's commitment to right thinking,
6. Enable the client to choose right behaviours,
7. Enable the client to enjoy feelings of significance and security.

Crabb's model also included a 3 Step programme that was designed to help any church identify and train gifted people to form a counselling team. Firstly he believed that everybody in the church should be trained to become a sensitive and caring listener. Secondly, a group of people who are mature in the faith should be selected for training that would help people tackle their problems from a Biblical perspective. Thirdly, from this group, a few people should be chosen to be trained in ways of helping those people who are struggling with deeper issues. If a programme like this was adopted, every Christian church would soon be able to offer a life-changing counselling service to the whole community.

Crabb saw the importance of helping people bring their thought processes into line with the way in which we have been designed by God and which is outlined in The Bible. He maintained that once this was achieved it would be possible for clients to choose more appropriate behaviours which would then begin to satisfy their feeling needs. A similar idea was taken up by Gary Collins, but in addition he identified that many mental and emotional problems can be linked to people having a dysfunctional self-image. He expanded on the Biblical concept of us being loved and valued unconditionally as children of the eternal God (Collins 1989) and added the need for 'self-belief'. He believed, for people's mental well-being, that it is essential for them to begin to see themselves in a way that is in line with the teachings of The Bible instead of what they had come to believe from what others around them have said.

Overall, the aim of Biblical counselling is to help people bring their lives into line with the teachings of The Bible and to become more Christ-like in attitude and behaviour. The process is based around helping each client to identify, challenge and change their negative, inaccurate thoughts and feelings and to substitute these with what The Bible has to say about them.

THEOTHERAPY (SPIRITUAL THERAPY)

There are many titles given to different types of spiritual therapy that might possibly come under the Christian umbrella (and many that do not), but it is not helpful to go into all of them here. A lot of them tend to follow a similar pattern which is linked to some aspect of inner healing and is very close to what we might refer to as 'prayer ministry', or even 'deliverance ministry'. Although exponents of these approaches would generally be happy to work with people of any faith, they all seem to include a priority about the client getting themselves right with God in a personal act of confession, repentance and complete surrender before proceeding. Therefore these approaches are much more suited to clients who are church people or those who already have a clear understanding of the Christian gospel message. The therapists are liable to be very directive in their approach with each session often conducted by two or three people who tend to maintain quite a strict level of control throughout the session and, sometimes, appear to do all the work.

Generally all the people who work in this way seem to have a strong belief that the supernatural power of God will resolve all the client's issues and this can often give the impression that the client really has little or nothing to do except simply to accept what they are told. The therapy is generally of a very personal nature and hinges mainly around acts of inner cleansing and inner healing. This involves confessing and releasing everything to God in an act of unconditional surrender and then receiving the supernatural power of The Holy Spirit.

There is plenty of evidence to suggest that this kind of therapy can be hugely successful for lots of people but it is absolutely imperative for everyone who wishes to receive this kind of ministry to check that their therapist(s) are under the authority of, and accountable to, a local Bible-believing Christian church and that they are adhering to an established protocol. Solo or isolated practitioners in this field are definitely to be avoided because they can do untold damage to vulnerable and unsuspecting people.

IN CONCLUSION

Anyone who wishes to obtain the services of a counsellor should check very thoroughly what they are being offered before they agree to begin the process and be extremely wary of any counsellor who is not prepared to provide a comprehensive answer to all your questions. This can be especially important when seeking a Christian Counsellor because there are many forms of Christian help which do not conform to the standards required to be recognised as counselling. We will look at some of these in the next chapter.

Whatever approach is being used, all counsellors should have a few basic principles in place to be able to practice ethically and should not mind being asked about these. In no particular order, here are some of the main elements which people should check:

- Their level of Training, Experience and Qualification,
- Their regular receipt of formal Counselling Supervision,
- Their Formal Working Agreement (or Contract),
- Their understanding and application of Confidentiality,
- Their level of appropriate Insurance cover,
- Their ability to maintain appropriate Boundaries,
- Their Complaints procedures,
- Their accountability to a nationally accepted Code of Ethics.

10

HOW DOES CHRISTIAN COUNSELLING COMPARE WITH OTHER FORMS OF CHRISTIAN HELPING ?

In order to see how Christian counselling compares with the wider aspects of what the Christian church might offer, it is helpful for us to consider some of the differences and some of the similarities of these elements and how they might complement one another. The Bible encourages every believer to use whatever gifts they possess to help others (1 Corinthians 12 v 28), and this is to be seen as a responsibility rather than an option, therefore people may find many different ways of doing this. What is listed here is not meant to be a comprehensive list of these opportunities, because there can be many adaptations and variations of these and others, but it is intended as an introduction to some of the most common forms of Christian helping that are available and how they differ from Christian counselling.

1. CHRISTIAN PASTORAL CARE

This Biblical principle, although adopted by many organisations, is really the prerogative of the Christian church and is generally a practical way of looking after people in order to ensure their needs are taken care of. It can include a very wide variety of activities ranging from occasional, casual contact to regular, structured meetings. It involves connecting with people who are going through particular times of difficulty as well as simply maintaining a link with people in order to give them a feeling of belonging.

Pastoral care can be demonstrated by making a telephone call, sending a card or letter, delivering flowers or a gift, providing fruit or a food parcel, sending an email or a text, or by making a personal visit. It is any form of encouragement that is given voluntarily and can be especially valuable for people who are sick or hospitalised. It could be a quick friendly chat or a long in-depth conversation.

Some of the practical forms of Pastoral Care may include taking on a specific job that someone is finding hard to undertake for themselves. This may include tasks such as: Painting and Decorating, Doing Odd Jobs or Repair Work, Gardening, Cleaning, Maintenance Work, Providing Transport, Shopping, Cooking, Financial Advice, Helping families with the Elderly or with Children, Running Errands, Filling Forms and so on. Enabling people to stay in touch with others by helping them get familiar with a Mobile telephone or with On-Line connections can also be a massive benefit.

There is a strong social element to pastoral care where, on many occasions, people just need someone to spend a little time with them. A friendly chat over a cup of tea will often fit the bill, or having someone who will share an activity or an interest. Most churches encourage their visitors to pray with the people they visit and perhaps read from The Bible because this also increases their sense of belonging and can strengthen their faith.

The predominant function of Pastoral Care is helping the people who may feel disadvantaged in some way, to feel they are not isolated or alone. This can often be accomplished through those who are willing to give of their skill, time and energy without any formal training. However, there are occasions where this type of help really needs to be coordinated in order to avoid anyone being overlooked. Such an additional level of efficiency will help to avoid any unnecessary duplication or confusion, and reduce any sense of the recipients feeling pressurised in any way.

Some organisations and churches may develop a process for people to request help in times of need and may have regular systems for keeping in touch with people. However, in most cases, the provision of Pastoral Care relies heavily on the awareness of neighbours, friends and family to bring their concerns to the attention of those in leadership of the organisation. This can enable the most appropriate action to be initiated and some form of follow-up managed so as to check whether the situation has been dealt with effectively.

2. CHRISTIAN TEACHING

This is the process of educating people by imparting knowledge of The Bible and its principles in a way that can be easily understood by the recipients. It is generally the responsibility of the Ministers, Pastors and those in Leadership of the church to handle this. However, it is quite common for others to be involved in teaching within the various organisations, groups and activities that operate within a church, but these people will normally be appointed by the church leaders according to their gifts and talents.

Most churches will have specific times and avenues through which their teaching is delivered, the most common of these are church services, home groups, youth groups, clubs and children's meetings. Most of the teaching will usually be based on a theme or a syllabus with the occasional 'hot topic' being addressed as the need arises. For most of these sessions there would normally be an open invitation to attend, subject to any specific requirements, and the sessions would be fairly formal in nature.

Teaching is aimed at equipping and preparing people to be able to stand strong in their faith through the trials and tribulations of everyday life. In church services it tends to be delivered in a lecture style format, although small groups and mid-week meetings will frequently engage in practical activities and lengthy discussions. They will also generally attempt to answer any questions that arise from within the group. Christian teaching is best presented by people who are trained and qualified to do this and regular sessions will often attract a following of regular attendees. Most churches occasionally need to call on enthusiastic amateurs to do their teaching and, although this can prove to be a great asset, the quality and content of the teaching may sometimes suffer as a result.

Christian Preaching is closely associated with teaching and can, equally, contain valuable information about Biblical principles. However, it usually includes the additional element of personal challenge in which people are encouraged, prompted and even urged to make a response. It tends to appeal, not just to the logical ability of its hearers, but to their hearts. Teaching requires little or no follow-up, whereas Preaching may require a follow-up to support those who have responded.

3. CHRISTIAN DISCIPLING

Christian disciples are people who are followers of Jesus and we have all been given a directive from Jesus to make more disciples wherever we go (Matthew 28 v 19). In discipling people we seek to emulate the way Jesus developed His followers through a combination of teaching, training, challenging, correcting, testing, stretching, modelling, caring and releasing. Although it is impossible for us to repeat exactly what Jesus did, we can attempt to reproduce elements of His unique style, even though we may want to introduce them with a modern slant. There are an infinite number of possible variations here and a great many resources are currently available in a wide variety of different formats. It does not really matter exactly how people are discipled, just as long as there are those who are prepared and willing to undertake the task.

Some people have been known to form life-long friendships following a period of discipleship training together and this is an indication of the nature of this type of training. It needs to be, of necessity, a close and personal relationship because it has implications for every aspect of a person's life and its aim is to give them a solid basis on which to build their faith for the future.

Lots of people, including church leaders, prefer to take potential disciples through a structured course to ensure that really important elements are not overlooked whereas others are happy to work on a more ad-hoc basis. Either way, this can be done with individuals or in small groups, but every person should be encouraged to continually ask questions as the programme progresses.

Discipleship programmes can be flexible, can be arranged at any time and in any convenient venue but should always be conducted by someone who is sufficiently experienced in the Christian faith that they are able to handle some challenging questions. It can be delivered by people without any specific training but facilitators should make sure they familiarise themselves with all the materials of the whole programme before beginning to work with anyone. It will usually require an on-going relationship to be established which helps to build up the recipient(s) over a period of time.

4. CHRISTIAN GUIDANCE

This may sometimes be referred to as Spiritual Direction and it amounts to someone who is in a position of authority giving advice, from a Biblical perspective, to another person regarding a particular issue. Such Guidance is normally sought by the recipient who would approach someone they trust and respect. Whenever Guidance is given without being requested it can come across as dictatorial or even domineering and is therefore much more likely to be rejected.

Christian Guidance is usually given in a relaxed, informal and confidential setting on a one-to-one basis. It is generally sought from people who are experienced in the Christian faith and who may have been through similar experiences themselves or have helped others who are facing a similar issue. It is not uncommon for people to seek Guidance from several mature people before settling on a decision of their own. It may require only a single conversation, although in the case of persistent issues the recipient may request regular contact over a period of time. Follow-up is not really required, although the person giving the Guidance will often want to know, as a matter of interest, if their advice was taken and whether the desired outcome was achieved by the recipient.

5. CHRISTIAN MENTORING

This form of support and encouragement is often overlooked in Christian circles but it can be a vital way of bringing on younger people in some aspect of their work and faith. It tends to be a long term relationship between two people, one with high levels of experience and one who wants to learn. It may relate to a specific activity or task, or be more about a general lifestyle development. Usually the one who wishes to learn will seek to emulate his Mentor and ask for regular feedback on his progress. It will usually involve meeting regularly to discuss the work and evaluate progress. A mentor aids the growth and development of another person through direct conversation and input based on their own experience and skill (Peck 2014).

Occasionally someone may be allocated to a Mentor in order to develop a particular set of skills and this is a widely accepted method for recognising those who may possess leadership potential. It is a valid way of training up gifted people and preparing them to take over a particular role at some point in the future or to expand the work by breaking new ground. Either way, this is a great way to increase the number of skilled personnel who are able to fill a particular role. It is my strong belief that every person in any form of Christian leadership should be mentoring someone with a view to passing some responsibility on to them at some point.

It is an ideal process for encouraging people to develop their spiritual gifts and skills in a way that allows them to experiment within a framework of accountability. It includes the opportunity to watch their Mentor at work, to work alongside their Mentor, to do the work under the watchful eye of their Mentor, and eventually to work alone. Follow-up would normally be continuous until such time as the person is released to work on their own.

6. CHRISTIAN COACHING

A coach seeks to facilitate the growth, development and progress of another person's skills and abilities by non-directive conversation, through their observation, challenge and feedback (Peck 2014). The Christian Coach is someone who has the skills to be able to tap into the spiritual desires and aspirations of others so that they feel motivated to move on to higher levels of personal achievement. There are many levels of coaching and many levels at which people might want to receive coaching. This means that it is best to be undertaken by someone who is formally trained and qualified, who understands different coaching models and approaches, and is able to select the most appropriate approach for each person in each situation. One popular system which can be used in a wide variety of situations is the GROWTH model which was developed by Growth Coaching International in Australia (see appendix).

Coaching is generally initiated by the person who wishes to receive the coaching for a specific purpose but occasionally someone might be singled out who is perceived to have real talent and who could benefit from receiving coaching. A specific agreement would then be sought between the two parties concerning the arrangements and terms that would work best for both of them, provided of course that there was complete agreement about the goals to be tackled. Coaching is most commonly conducted on a one-to-one basis but could be offered to a group of like-minded individuals who have similar objectives. Christian Coaching could be helpful in a wide variety of disciplines including such things as; preaching, teaching, prayer ministry and all aspects of leadership.

7. CHRISTIAN MEDIATION

Mediation is the act of helping to resolve difficulties between two parties when their relationship has broken down. It can relate to issues that occur in marriage, in business, in families, in organisations, between neighbours, or between friends. It is sometimes referred to as conflict management because it is usually called upon as a result of serious disagreements or differences and frequently hinges around a lack of appropriate communication skills.

Whilst a request for mediation will often come from only one party, it is essential to obtain the agreement of both parties before the commencement of any action. This must be done by the mediator, or facilitator, to ensure that both parties are willing to accept his ability to be completely impartial. Anyone who is a trusted and respected third party could act as a mediator but it is better to appoint someone who has the training and experience to know how to handle situations like this.

All meetings should be confidential and held in private. The first step is for the mediator to meet each party separately and individually to get a thorough grasp of their understanding of the situation. Comprehensive notes should be taken with the full agreement of everyone involved before attempting to bring the parties together.

Inexperienced Christians will be tempted to simply quote verses from The Bible as a means of resolving the conflict or ask people to go away and pray about it. This is rarely effective because it shows a lack of any real understanding of the issues involved or of each person's perception of it. Good mediation involves the skills to seek a 'win-win' situation by establishing clear links with each party's core values and beliefs before moving on to discuss the development of mutual forgiveness or formal agreement.

The Bible explains that we have a mediator between mankind and God, the person of Jesus Christ (1 Timothy 2 v 5), which tells us that God's heart is for all differences between us to be completely reconciled so that we can live in harmony together. Christian principles indicate that we should exercise a similar responsibility towards one another (2 Corinthians 5 v 18 – 20).

8. CHRISTIAN TRAINING

The principle of Christian Training is different to Teaching because it has a practical connotation attached to it and aims to provide a time of specifically focused activity that will prepare people to be better equipped for the future. It will usually involve a structured programme, or course, which has a combination of theory and practice in a specific subject and would be presented by someone with the appropriate qualifications and experience. Where possible, any form of Christian Training should be accredited by an external organisation so that the resultant qualification can be independently recognised.

There is a large amount of Christian Training that takes place within existing church structures and serves to equip its members to be more effective in a particular role. Such courses may be open to any of the members or be by invitation only but will tend to form a part of the overall programme of the church and be linked to its vision and mission. In addition, there are many para-church organisations who run their own training programmes in their specialist subjects. These may or may not be formally accredited externally, but generally serve to widen the experience of those who take part.

In the current spiritual climate, there is a great need for high quality training in every aspect of Christian work, and for more of this to be formally accredited and recognised by the world at large. This will help to build trust and credibility with the wider public and help to remove any suspicion about our motives. In this way, what the church has to offer is more likely to be accepted by the secular world and this will make it easier for Christians to break down barriers and make a significant impact within their local communities and beyond.

9. CHRISTIAN CONSULTANCY OR SUPERVISION

Within the counselling profession it is seen as an essential ingredient for every counsellor to be receiving regular, formal counselling supervision, and this may sometimes be referred to as consultancy. Absolutely no-one is deemed to be outside this requirement so it produces a commonly accepted element which is aimed at creating and maintaining the highest standards of practice for everyone. It is a way of making every individual counsellor accountable to a common Code of Ethics, regardless of where they practice, and it provides a non-threatening way of keeping everyone up to date. Since this has become accepted as normal practice within counselling every person is made accountable to someone. In this way the whole profession benefits and each person is able to be regularly challenged about their levels of self care and ways of working effectively.

Many organisations and businesses have introduced a similar system in order to maintain their own standards and monitor the effectiveness of their staff, but this is not to be confused with 'line management' nor to be seen as a 'big brother' exercise just to check up on everyone. When it is being done correctly it will include elements of training and education, of support and encouragement, and of structure and competence.

Unfortunately lots of church leaders consider systems like this to be 'worldly' and not consistent with the teachings of Scripture. However, The Bible is clear, we are required to submit to <u>one another</u> out of reverence for Christ (Ephesians 5 v 21). Without doing this, we can all miss out on the advantages that come from regular contact, such as the encouragement of each individual and an improvement in levels of communication. The accurate dissemination of information and the quick reception of feedback are essential to the development of every successful organisation, and churches are no different. These are the things that can make each person feel they are important, and they can be easily implemented when a good supervision system is put in place. Churches could be setting an example for others to follow by adopting a system like this which demonstrates that every person is important and that their views are valued.

Christian Supervision could become part of the culture of every Christian organisation and church by encouraging each person to make themselves accountable on a regular basis to someone they trust and respect. This would have particular benefit for those who hold positions of leadership or specific areas of responsibility. Suggestions could be made as to what form the meetings should take and the kind of issues that could be discussed so as to be of mutual benefit. Important information can be passed out quickly, new ideas and programmes can be discussed, policies and procedures can be updated, and everyone can be given the opportunity to make a valid contribution.

Whilst no specific qualifications are necessary for this role, people could be encouraged to link up with someone who will challenge any inertia and promote constant progress towards greater levels of spiritual maturity. Of course, this can appear to be very time consuming, but when every person is actively involved and can see it as an important part of both their personal and corporate development, it can become a pathway to real growth for everyone.

10. CHRISTIAN PRAYER MINISTRY

Whilst prayer should be a normal everyday occurrence for every Christian, there are some who have a gift, or ministry, of praying for the needs of others. Prayer is generally thought of as the way we bring our needs to the attention of Almighty God and, although this is quite appropriate, there is an aspect to prayer that is much more significant than this. It is not just the process of asking God to intervene in our trials and tribulations but of using every situation to bring our lives into line with His plans and purposes and of hearing what He has to say to us. People who move in this kind of ministry have developed an ability to hear God and are able to relate this to the people for whom they are praying. This then becomes more than simply bringing a shopping list of requests to God, but of hearing from Him about what we need to do and the things we need to change in order to be more open to receive all that He has to give us.

People who move in this ministry usually have a prophetic gifting which also enables them to speak out what God is saying. They can sometimes be referred to as a Seer. This gives us a clue about how to recognise them by the way they use this gift: it is never critical, condemning or judgemental but always **S**trengthening, **E**ducational, **E**ncouraging and **R**eassuring (1 Corinthians 14 v 3).

Prayer ministry should not only be about praying for those who ask for it, but it should be an opportunity to teach people how to pray and how to make their praying more effective. Many people would rather ask someone else to pray for them than to do it for themselves. Many also think that God is more likely to hear if the praying is done by someone who is more accomplished at it. There are a great many myths about prayer but the bottom line is that God actually wants everyone to communicate with Him so that He has the opportunity to communicate with them. This can be a bit frightening for those who are not familiar with prayer so it can involve beginning to break down any barriers that exist and of correcting any misconceptions people may have about God.

11. CHRISTIAN HEALING

The life of Jesus, as recorded in the Gospels, gives us a clear indication that God has a real desire to heal people, but it is possible to have quite a distorted view of what this actually means and be uncertain about how the Christian church should be involved. Our human perspective predisposes us to put more emphasis on physical healing, but when God talks about sickness He is referring not just to physical healing, but to mental, emotional and spiritual healing as well (Mark 5 v 15). His main concern is that we should live in close relationship to Him and, as a result of this, receive all of His promises to enjoy the health and abundance He provides. This is borne out by one of the names through which God originally wanted His people to know Him - Jehovah Rophe, which means "I am The Lord who heals you" (Exodus 15 v 26).

Although Jesus ministered predominantly to Jews, He did not make it a requirement of people to conform to Jewish traditions or customs in order to be healed. He often commended people just for having faith in Him, He sometimes asked people what they really wanted to receive from Him, and He often asked people to respond by taking a step of faith, but He never demanded anything from them in order to be healed. He did it all to awaken people's interest in, and awareness of, the kingdom of heaven.

When He initially commissioned His disciples, He sent them out with the power and authority to heal people as a practical way of demonstrating the reality of their preaching about the kingdom of God (Luke 9 v 1-2 and 10 v 1). Then, among the final words He spoke to His followers was His command to go into the whole world to preach the gospel and to encourage every believer to demonstrate the power of God by healing the sick (Mark 16 v 15-18).

We can understand from this therefore, that it is a Christian responsibility to offer God's healing power to people who request it, under the direct guidance of the Lord, whatever their condition may be and regardless of their background. This should not be considered as taking the place of sound medical advice and treatment, because we recognise that these are also provided by our sovereign creator God. In fact, it should become general practice whenever someone receives healing through the power of God that they are encouraged to immediately consult their doctor for a medical check up by way of confirmation.

The commission from Jesus indicates that every believer has been given the authority to work in this way, but Scripture also indicates that some people are given specific supernatural 'gifts of healings' through The Holy Spirit (1 Corinthians 12 v 9). This seems to show that even though different gifts are given to people for different kinds of healing, all are to be administered through the exercising of faith. It also indicates that no particular training or qualification is required other than to be filled with The Holy Spirit. However, churches and Christian organisations should offer opportunities for people to prepare themselves by learning how to improve their sensitivity to God's voice and how to exercise appropriate protocols for administering God's healing.

12. CHRISTIAN DELIVERANCE

This is often believed to be a specialist area of ministry which relates to releasing people from the influence of demonic forces. These forces may appear in the lives of people as a form of severe oppression or as a controlling power from which they feel unable to break free. This is not a trivial matter and should never be treated flippantly, but it should also not be magnified out of proportion. The Bible teaches that every follower of

Jesus is able to call on the supernatural power of His Holy Spirit to dispel any forces of evil (Matthew 10 v 8, Mark 16 v 17, Luke 10 v 17). However, it must be understood that demonic forces are far more powerful than we are and so dispatching them can only be achieved in the name of the living Lord Jesus Christ as The Holy Spirit flows through someone who is a fully surrendered believer. This means that it is incredibly difficult for anyone to do this for themselves or on their own.

There is no magic formula for breaking this kind of oppression, and it can be administered by any individual Christian, but it is best undertaken by someone; who is mature in the teaching of The Bible on these matters, who is familiar with moving under the promptings of the Holy Spirit, and who is accompanied by someone of a like mind. People who ask for this kind of release should be helped to explore the sources of their oppression and also be taught how to receive the fullness of The Holy Spirit in order to prevent any similar experiences from re-occurring.

13. CHRISTIAN SELF-HELP GROUPS

The idea of self-help groups is not a new one, but it is one in which few churches seem to appreciate the advantages. The philosophy is that when a group of people who are grappling with a similar issue commit themselves to meet together regularly, they are able to be an encouraging resource for one another. Groups can be of any size, but work best when between 8 and 10 people meet with a facilitator. This aims to ensure that each person is given the opportunity both to contribute and to receive, and that the overall focus of the group can be maintained.

Some groups allow people to drop in whenever they feel the need, but the most effective way of working is when the same people agree to meet over a specific period of time so that a relationship of trust can be built and confidentiality can be maintained. Facilitators should be people who are skilled in their understanding of group dynamics and be experienced in the Christian faith but should not seek to dictate the process.

There are great benefits to be obtained when a person chooses to make themselves accountable to a group of their peers in this way. The advantages of being understood by others who are going through similar experiences and of exploring together the most effective ways of moving forward should not be underestimated.

14. CHRISTIAN SOCIAL ACTIVITY

Christian churches should always be ready to take advantage of any opportunity to serve their local community as well as to provide social interaction and activity for their own members. There are many ways in which this can be done, depending upon the situation, the premises, the resources available and the skills of the people.

The possibilities are endless, but some of the most commonly adopted activities include: providing meals for the needy, work with the homeless, night shelters, foodbanks, professional financial advice, parents and toddlers groups, support for missionaries and overseas workers, fitness groups, drop-in centres, cafes, arts and crafts groups, music and/or choirs, board games evenings, litter picks, maintaining public spaces and gardens, support for local charities, and liaison with local councils and elected representatives. The possibilities are endless.

FINALLY

Whatever programmes or activities are offered under the auspices of the Christian church it is essential to ensure that all the correct health and safety measures are followed, that local bye-laws are respected, and that people with appropriate qualifications and skills are involved in the planning and delivery of such services in every case. It is a false economy to skimp on any of these and it could result in major problems surfacing which are likely to have a negative impact on the Christian witness.

11

THE WAVERLEY MODEL

It is a commonly accepted fact that the foundational view any counsellor holds regarding the nature of mankind is going to determine the way they approach their counselling. When Selwyn Hughes began to develop his 5-Circle model for counselling, he took his understanding of the nature of man from The Bible and made it clear that without this knowledge of how people are designed, how they function, and how they perform, any approach to counselling will be little more than a friendly conversation. He maintained that Christian counselling must be rooted, grounded and guided by the teachings of The Bible, so he took 1 Thessalonians 5 v 23 as an example that identified all humans as tri-partite beings who are made in the image of God. He then adopted the common understanding that the soul of man consists of his mind, will and emotions, and these, along with the human spirit and the physical body make up the whole person. Thus he identified five distinct areas of human functioning which he entitled:

Spiritual, Rational, Volitional, Emotional, Physical,

and he defined them in this way:

1. The Spiritual element is the motivating part of the person which is designed to function most effectively when in constant communion with The Holy Spirit. It is the area in which our most crucial needs appear and these, if not fully met, will produce

debilitating spiritual and psychological issues which will interfere with every other area of human functioning.
2. The Rational element is the capability we have to think, reason, and comprehend. It is this ability that determines how we perceive the world around us and how we react to it. When our thinking is flawed it can have drastic consequences for the functioning of our whole being and will affect the choices and decisions we make.
3. The Volitional element is the ability we have to exercise our will. We are able to make choices and decisions about how we wish to move forward or respond to situations and circumstances. Although we have been given the freedom of choice, our decisions are strongly motivated by our deep inner desires (or goals), however, we are unable to have any influence over the consequences of our choices. Flawed choices will produce debilitating and damaging effects in every area of human functioning.
4. The Emotional element is what enables us to experience or to 'feel' the world around us. Our feelings play a vital part in our ability to enjoy life and to appreciate things. Dominant emotions (those that regularly recur) can create problems in every other area of human functioning and allow the difficulties to remain longer than they should.
5. The Physical element is the way in which we engage with the world around us, primarily through our five senses. It is also the way in which we recognise when something is not right for us, either internally or externally. In other words, we can experience pain or become aware of other more subtle physiological changes.

By using this '5 Circle' approach counsellors are able to incorporate a wide variety of different psychological tools into a thoroughly investigative style of counselling that can help a person identify and deal with the source of their issues. Selwyn describes the role of the Christian Counsellor as someone who is able to help each client determine which of their areas of functioning contain problematic issues, to identify them specifically, and then work with them to correct these by bringing them into line with the Word of God. To help people understand this process he created the 5-Circle diagram which shows the five areas as concentric circles beginning with the outer Physical circle and progressing through the Emotional, Volitional, and Rational circles, to finish with the Spiritual circle in the centre.

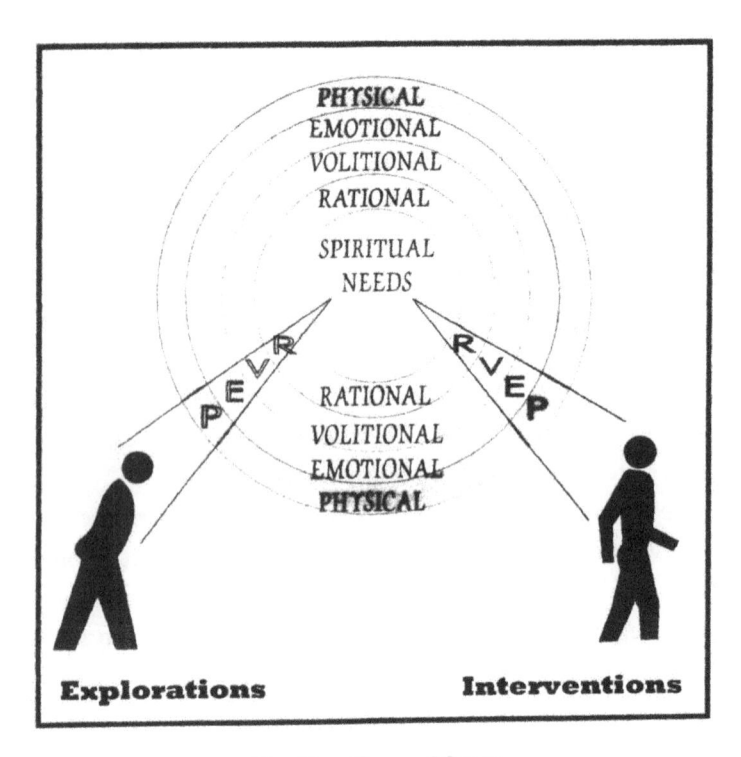

THE FIVE CIRCLE MODEL

The Christian Counsellor should explain this outline carefully to each client prior to the commencement of counselling and encourage them to ask any questions they may have. He should then adopt the following Three-Phase approach (AIR) to begin the therapeutic process itself: Assess, Investigate, Resolve.

> <u>The Assessment Phase</u> is a fact gathering exercise where the client is encouraged to describe in as much detail as possible why they are asking for counselling and what they would like to achieve from it. This is the time when the counsellor discovers as much as possible about the background of the client and the circumstances they are encountering at that time.

<u>The Investigation Phase</u> is where counsellor and client work inwards together through the five circles one at a time. They spend time in each circle seeking to identify and label any problematic issues, uncovering the triggers, exposing what is helping to maintain them, and looking for any repetitive patterns of behaviour.

<u>The Resolution Phase</u> is the process where the counsellor and client work together to move outwards through the five circles, one at a time, whilst attempting to establish specific ways of applying Biblical principles at every stage.

The most crucial stage of therapy is reached on the inward journey when arriving at the Spiritual circle. Here clients are faced with the task of identifying their own values and beliefs which will expose the ways in which they are seeking to get their core needs met. The greatest challenge for the counsellor at this point is to explain how the client's core needs can, in reality, only be fully met through a personal relationship with Jesus Christ. Great care must be exercised to explain the spiritual principles at this point without pressurising the client in any way. It will often require much time to be spent here until the client has a thorough understanding and is able to make a reasoned choice before proceeding.

THE COUNSELLING PROCESS

We are now going to look in more detail at each stage of the counselling process using the Waverley model and consider how it can become a most effective strategy for helping people regardless of their faith, background, or beliefs.

<u>(A) The Assessment Phase</u>

The assessment phase begins when the very first contact is made with a client. This will often come in the form of a telephone call or an email where the client is requesting information about the counselling style or approach used and how the counselling process will work. Other issues will also need to be discussed including venue, timings, payments and the need for a formal contract, or working agreement, to be agreed before the commencement of any sessions. At this point the counsellor (or initial contact person) will obtain important contact details from the client and an indication of the issues they would like to raise in counselling. Even through these fairly general discussions a lot of valuable information can be gained about the client and this should be recorded on an 'Initial Contact' form that is to be kept in the counsellor's client file.

At this point it is usual for some of the practical issues about counselling to be explained to the client along with the need for a formal contract, or working agreement, to be put in place. My personal preference at this stage is for me to arrange an informal chat with each potential client so that I can go through each clause of my 'Working Agreement' (Contract) prior to the first counselling session. This gives my client the opportunity to check me out, to ask any questions they wish, and for me to get an impression of how they might respond to counselling. My intention is to put my client completely at ease and enable them to come to the first session prepared and ready to begin the therapy. I usually give them a copy of my contract to take away (or send one to them) so they can seek advice or support from others if necessary before signing it and giving it back to me before the first session begins. This allows for a sort of cooling off period and makes it easy for people to decide not to begin therapy if they are not really ready. It also clears up any misunderstandings about what happens in counselling and lets them know that I don't give advice, suggest what they should do, tell them what I would do, or talk about my own experiences.

Once the first session commences the main emphasis of the counsellor should be to establish a sound working relationship and this will involve making a strong empathic connection with the client. As the session progresses it is likely to involve a lot of explanations about various aspects of the counselling process and the counsellor should be using all his skills to encourage the client to speak freely and openly at all times. The counsellor has the responsibility to manage each session effectively and should take notes throughout. Many inexperienced counsellors struggle with the idea of taking notes while the client is speaking but it is essential to jot down brief comments and key words as they arise. These can be written up more fully when the session has ended, but to not write anything until that point is almost certain to guarantee that important details will be missed. I learned this lesson very early in my counselling career when I got the family details of one client confused with the details of another client I was working with at the same time. It was embarrassing and unprofessional and it caused my client to be more cautious for a while about what he shared with me.

There are a wide variety of outlines, formats, record sheets and questionnaires which may be helpful in gaining a wider appreciation of the circumstances under which the client is seeking counselling, but these should never be introduced without explanation or without the approval of the client. Whilst they can produce a valuable source of background information, at this stage they should only be treated as a guide to understanding the presenting problems and a possible route to deeper issues that could be explored later. One way of doing this is to work through the client's 10 Basic Life Areas.

The 10 Basic Life Areas

PHASE 1:   INITIAL EXPLORATION

1. Marital &/or Family Relationships

2. Social &/or Friendly Relationships

3. Occupation and Employment (inc. Voluntary work)

4. Finances (Inc. Debts etc.)

5. Spiritual Life and Experience

6. Sexual Activity

7. Recreational Activity

8. Physical Health (including medical history)

9. Leisure Activity (including use of stimulants)

10. Routine Responsibilities

(Adapted from Selwyn Hughes 1990)

THE 10 BASIC LIFE AREAS

(I) The Investigation Phase

This is the point where counsellor and client begin to work inwards through each of the five circles to specifically identify and record the problematic issues in each circle and to draw up a kind of diagnosis. There will be a massive temptation, as each circle is opened up, to want to deal with some of the issues straight away, but it must be stressed to the client that this is just the beginning of the investigation stage and it is not until a full picture of the client's issues emerges that the process of addressing these can properly begin. Inexperienced counsellors will find this very difficult to resist but in order for the therapy to be effective it is essential to be able to see the whole picture before any possible solutions are considered. The most destructive opinions about the counselling profession are generated as a result of well-meaning people, who call themselves counsellors, trying to help clients resolve their problems before they have a comprehensive understanding of what is involved and without seeing the issues from the client's perspective. Working with the symptoms alone, however helpful that might initially appear, must never be regarded as an effective way of offering counselling.

THE PHYSICAL CIRCLE INVESTIGATION

As humans, we have been made in the image of God and placed within a physical frame. If this frame is not working properly it will have a detrimental effect on the whole person by interfering with our ability to function in each of the five areas. In fact, we must be aware that physical difficulties can create such a negative influence that people may believe they are incapable of change. Any physical conditions, whether temporary or permanent, should be fully discussed at this point. Sharp powers of observation and an inquisitive mind will be the counsellor's best tools whilst working in this Circle.

The objective in this Circle therefore, is to determine whether there are any physical problems that are negatively influencing the client's attitudes, moods, or other aspects of their functioning. This should always include a thorough review of any medications and/or treatments the client is receiving along with a detailed discussion about anything the client may be doing to alleviate or avoid any physical issues.

An informal discussion about each of the 10 Basic Life Areas will be a great asset and should be included at this point with brief notes taken for possible further exploration later. It might also be helpful to complete a client risk assessment form before moving on. All information should be accurately recorded and kept confidentially for future reference in the counsellor's client file.

THE EMOTIONAL CIRCLE INVESTIGATION

Lots of people grow up learning how to hide their emotions. They can learn how to repress them, which is to hold them in check, or to suppress them which is to deny them or bury them. It is only when we are able to acknowledge and own our emotions that we will be able to manage them effectively. Most of our emotions are produced as a result of our evaluation of life experiences (see E+E=E diagram on page 55). This means that two people who may be in the same situation but evaluate it differently, can consequently experience a range of quite different emotions. Emotions can be either positive or negative, but from a counselling point of view we are concerned primarily with those that are negative and dysfunctional because if these get buried they will continue to fester under the surface and then generate harmful responses which could surface without warning.

All emotions are vital signals of something that is going on internally for us and they often indicate that something has changed internally. They should never be ignored and therefore the objective in this circle is to get the client to acknowledge all their negative emotions and to identify the dominant ones. The counsellor must maintain a strong empathic connection with his client here because this will become an essential ingredient for effective work going forward. Time that is spent with great care and accuracy in this circle will create a powerful platform for the work ahead.

We must now understand some vital differences between the ways a person might respond to someone they wish to help and see that, for the counsellor, there is no substitute for a strong empathic connection.

> Sympathy is feeling _like_ the other person and suffering with them
> Affinity is believing that your feelings are _the same as_ the other person
> Pity is feeling sorry _for_ the other person but choosing to do nothing
> Empathy is feeling _with_ the other person but maintaining objectivity

It is only the sensitivity of the counsellor at this point that will enable the client to talk about their most difficult and painful emotions but this will require the counsellor to accurately experience something of what the client is experiencing and, without being overwhelmed, to relate this back to him. This begins with the counsellor making a real effort to see things in the way his client is seeing them and to feel something of what his client is feeling, but then encouraging his client to identify and name the feelings for himself.

Our emotions are generated internally as a direct response to how we perceive our ability to achieve our goals. When any strong negative emotions are denied or remain unmanaged they will produce further problems for us in the future. The most problematic and dysfunctional emotions are: Anger, Anxiety, Fear and Guilt.

Anger is usually the result of a goal that becomes blocked or Undermined
Anxiety is usually the result of a goal that is vague - or Uncertain
Fear is usually the result of a goal that is threatening - or Unsafe
Guilt is usually the result of a goal that is too far off - or Unreachable.

Helping the client to keep a record of his negative emotions can prove a great asset as the counselling progresses. He should be encouraged to note both the frequency and the intensity of his experiences as they happen so as to build up a factual picture of his own responses over a period of time. This can later provide valuable evidence to the client of the progress that is being made.

THE VOLITIONAL CIRCLE INVESTIGATION

This circle focuses on the ability we all possess to exercise our Will and to make choices and decisions about our goals. All our responses, whether verbal, emotional or behavioural, are choices which are motivated by our desire to achieve a goal. A vital part of the therapeutic process therefore, must be to discover and identify the client's goals which have been generated by his thought processes. Behind most of the problems our clients are facing will be an inappropriate and unhelpful goal.

We have all been given the freedom to make our own choices and therefore will have chosen certain goals for ourselves that we believe will be able to satisfy our core needs. The role of the counsellor here is to help his client identify specifically the goals he has chosen, being guided by the emotions that were identified in the previous circle. Where a dominant emotion was uncovered, there is likely to be a dominant goal to be explored but, once again this process cannot be rushed. It may take a while for the client to grasp the connection between his emotions, his choices and his goals, and to appreciate that this is still just a part of the data-gathering exercise you are engaged in as you continue to work inwards through the five circles. However, it is essential to clearly identify the client's key goals at this stage, and not to proceed without achieving this.

There will frequently be recurring patterns of responses and behaviours so it can be helpful to get the client to keep a diary or a journal to this effect. The advantage of this is that it allows the client to notice his own patterns of responses and then to review this evidence within the counselling sessions. This can be a hard undertaking for most clients and will generally require a great deal of patient coaching on the part of the counsellor before usable information is produced. Moving gently but purposely through this circle will help to prevent the client becoming exasperated and will set important precedents for moving into the next Circle.

THE RATIONAL CIRCLE INVESTIGATION

Man's God-given ability to think and to reason is an extraordinary quality but we must appreciate that this does not make us infallible. Although we are able to apply logic to thinking and making plans, we are in fact, seriously flawed in this respect because we are only able to perceive the world through the imperfect and tainted lens of our personal understanding and experience. This tends to produce, and to sustain, inaccurate thoughts and assumptions which then dominate the choices we make. One difficulty here is that we get used to our own attempts to structure our world in ways that make sense to us. As a result, we can fail to realise how much this increases the likelihood of becoming immune to any other perceptions and it can convince us that we really do know what is best for ourselves.

It is the internal words we constantly choose to say to ourselves that actually create and sustain many of our problems. Thus, our thinking, even though frequently faulty and irrational, determines the choices we make. Since the brain is the control centre of the human body, every response whether verbal, emotional or behavioural must be preceded by a thought and many of these will be habitually negative and dysfunctional because they are based on our own faulty beliefs. Therefore the role of the therapist in the Rational Circle is to help his client expose and identify all forms of wrong thinking and self-talk. This can be compared to tunes that are continually running through our heads like CDs on replay but it is the constant repetition which forces our opinions and beliefs to become indelibly ingrained.

Most clients will quickly be able to recognise that they have many positive and helpful thoughts so the counsellor or psychotherapist should explain that the therapeutic process is concerned primarily with those thoughts that are negative. These are often referred to among CBT practitioners as NATs, or Negative Automatic Thoughts, and the exercise to identify is them labelled 'Trap the NATs'. At first, it is quite common for clients to believe they don't have any thoughts at all prior to making a response, or that their responses are almost instinctive. It can sometimes take a while for clients to get used to the concept of identifying these thoughts and it may require a number of attempts to get them into the habit of doing this. There are various processes, forms, or exercises which the therapist might use to assist the client with this and it could be helpful initially to treat it as a bit of a game but without losing sight of the more serious implications.

It is what we think, and what we tell ourselves about a situation, that determines our emotions and how we feel. So identifying and stating clearly the negative and irrational thoughts we are entertaining is a vital aspect of the work in this Circle. These thoughts will all be based on the strong belief that we know best and are capable of making our own decisions that will satisfy our Core Needs.

THE SPIRITUAL CIRCLE INVESTIGATION

Whether we believe it or not, we have all been created as spiritual beings with deep desires and longings. Some people who find this hard to accept may find it easier to understand that every person possess a spiritual dimension and that in order to understand human nature the counsellor must take this into account. It is here that our crucial core needs for Security, Significance and Self-Worth must be met. Every person will strive to have these needs met in one way or another and this is likely to lead them to adopt some strange and unusual patterns of behaviour. The role of the counsellor at this point is to help his client determine exactly what they are doing to meet these Core Needs. It is so vital to have these needs met that powerful internal drives are produced which can dominate every aspect of the personality and make it appear completely normal to behave in this way.

Staying with the investigation process at this point requires time and patience to consider each of these core needs in some detail until the specific actions of the client concerning each one have been identified. This will generally include getting the client to speak about ways they may have been labelled, hurt and rejected at an early age and what they have done, and may still be doing, to compensate for this. Specific challenges should be used here for each of the three core needs, for example: 'When do you feel most/least secure?', 'What do you look to for your security?', 'What is it that makes you feel most/least significant?', 'What makes you feel most/least good about yourself?'

It is a fact that nearly all the significant problems people experience in their lives originate with these core needs in their spiritual dimension so great care and sensitivity must be exercised here. Problem areas can only be faced and resolved once they have been exposed so the counsellor must be extremely careful not to skim over anything too quickly but to stay with the exploration for as long as it takes. Once a detailed analysis is completed of what the client is doing to meet their own needs of Security, Significance and Self-Worth the counsellor should present a summary of all the problematic issues that have been identified as a result of the Investigation journey inwards through the Five Circles to this point. The client is now ready to commence the Resolution phase which begins in the Spiritual Circle and works outwards through the Rational, Volitional, and Emotional to the Physical Circle.

(R) <u>The Resolution Phase</u>

The counsellor will now be in possession of notes about all the problematic areas the client identified as they worked inwards through each of the five circles during the Investigation Phase. Using these notes, the counsellor is now in a position to help his client begin addressing each one of these in turn as together they work out through the five circles. This process of correction and application must be approached equally carefully and sensitively, without any pressure being applied by the counsellor. Although there will be aspects of explanation required here, it must be a process in which the client makes his own choices. The counsellor must resist the temptation to tell his client what to do and encourage him to make his own discoveries and plan his own programme of implementation for every step. A key maxim to keep in mind now is:-

What a person is told to do can quickly be forgotten, but what they make as a personal discovery, will always be remembered.

The greatest of care must now be exercised with regard to the appropriate use both of the Scriptures and of Prayer from this point on. The resolution phase is not a licence to fall into the trap of dictating to a client, nor to abuse the relationship of trust which has been established up to this point. The inappropriate use of Scripture and Prayer will quickly destroy any empathic connection, will frequently bring the counselling process to a swift end, and will usually become a major block in the client's willingness to apply any of the resolutions. Whenever this happens, it will always be because the counsellor has lost sight of his objective and replaced it with his own desires. It is never the counsellor's responsibility to change his client, nor to persuade him to change, however attractive that prospect might be. Inappropriate actions of this nature will actually impede the work of The Holy Spirit and disrespect the autonomy of the client.

THE SPIRITUAL CIRCLE RESOLUTIONS

Before any resolution work can begin it is vital for the counsellor to explain once more the principles of the 5 Circle model. Diagrams, drawings and charts can be really useful at this point to ensure the client gets a clear picture of how the whole process works. Because the human spirit is designed to be in relationship to God, people will continue to experience spiritual and psychological problems in direct proportion to the degree their core needs are not being met by God in the spiritual dimension. He is the only way these needs can be fully satisfied so we become able to function to our true potential. People who choose to ignore God in this respect will constantly struggle to find alternative resources and will continue to demonstrate their own desire to be independent of Him by attempting to meet these needs themselves. Only when the spiritual realm is restored and re-aligned directly to God will people be able to deal comprehensively with the issues that arise in this and each of the other areas.

This is the point at which the counsellor must be able to present a clear picture of exactly _how_ God is able to meet our needs for Security, Significance and Self-Worth in a way that nothing else and no-one else ever can. It will be helpful to have a selection of Scriptures prepared in advance to explain how the human personality can only function correctly when its Core Needs are being fully met through a personal relationship with God. The counsellor will need to depend on the guidance and presence of The Holy Spirit and draw on the words of The Bible to be able to do this effectively. For example:-

> Security begins with a complete confidence in who I am, where I came from and where I am going; it is knowing that I am loved and wanted by someone who will never reject me and will never fail me.
> (Romans 5 v 8, Romans 8 v 31-38, 1 John 3 v 1)

> Significance is a clear understanding that my life has real meaning and importance, and that I have a specific

purpose in this life which underpins my whole existence.
(Ephesians 2 v 10, 1 John 3 v 1, 1 John 4v 10)

Self-Worth is the realisation that I am loved and valued unconditionally as an individual in my own right, not for what I can do, but for who I am.
(Psalm 139, Matthew 11 v 28, John 3 v 16)

The Roman Road to Christian Living
(One example from the book of Romans, in The Bible)

How to move from darkness to light, from death to life and from bondage to freedom.

1. **We are all sinners** — Romans 3 v 9 - 23
   Recognise that no-one is any better than anyone else

2. **We all deserve death** — Romans 6 v 23
   Acknowledge the consequences of our sinfulness

3. **We will all be Judged** — Romans 2 v 5 - 12
   Know that God is completely impartial

4. **We need to repent for sins** — Romans 2 v 4
   Realise the prompting of God's kindness and patience

5. **God has paid our debt** — Romans 5 v 6 - 8
   Understand how God demonstrated His love for us

6. **Have faith in Jesus** — Romans 3 v 22 - 26
   Choose to trust in God's promised righteousness

7. **Receive Peace and Joy** — Romans 5 v 1 - 5
   Accept the free gifts of God through His Son, Jesus

8. **Get Baptised** — Romans 6 v 1 - 8
   Take action to follow Jesus in acts of obedience

9. **Be filled with The Holy Spirit** — Romans 8 v 1 - 16
   Receive God's strength mentally, physically and spiritually

10. **Grow in Faith and Practice** — Romans 12 v 1 – 21
    Live by The Spirit and no longer by the standards of the world

If you to walk with God on a daily basis you will experience whole new dimensions of life as you keep responding to His promptings.

THE ROMAN ROAD

It is important to demonstrate that this is not just a matter of opinion but of factual evidence which is recorded in The Bible. The Scriptures make it clear that any behaviour where we turn our back on what God has done for us is classed as sin. Furthermore, He tells us there are only two sins that we have committed: firstly, we ignore His provision, and secondly, we rely on our own inadequate provision (Jeremiah 2 v 13). The counsellor should encourage his client to read these and other appropriate verses for himself from an accurate modern translation. This may create an opportunity for the client to take a step of faith he has never taken before by inviting Jesus to become his Saviour and Lord, so the whole process must be carefully documented and the full consent of the client obtained at every step. It is absolutely essential that no pressure of any sort is applied to the client during this process.

It is possible that other discussions may arise at this point, about prayer for example, or the authority of The Bible, or about the Christian life generally. Every question from the client should be taken seriously and answered comprehensively by the counsellor without being allowed to detract from the progress of the session. The counsellor must be ready to provide appropriate information for his client and to refer him for specific help from others where this might be necessary. Once again, any temptation to simply give instructions, to lecture, or to preach must be firmly resisted.

Full resolution within the spiritual circle will only happen when the client is willing to completely surrender himself to God and to receive the supernatural power of The Holy Spirit into his life with regard to each of his three Core Needs. This may require the counsellor to spend time gently explaining this process and to have appropriate materials available to support and encourage his client in each step. The essence of this stage is for the client to step down from the throne of his own life and re-instate God in His rightful place. It must be sensitively pointed out that the client will not be able to receive any assurance over these issues if he chooses to seek satisfaction and fulfilment from any other source.

A spiritual violation, or sin, cannot be corrected by simply trying to do better, but only by a specific act of confession and repentance. In this respect it is important to remember that confession is merely the acknowledgement of a wrongdoing, whereas repentance is making the decision to completely break with the old attitudes and behaviours in order to walk in God's ways from here on. This can be a good moment to encourage the client to confess and repent of any other sins. The counsellor should have an appropriate prayer written out for clients to use if they wish, although it is always better to encourage people to use their own words if at all possible, even if a little guidance is required here.

Becoming a Christian Counsellor

An example of a prayer of confession and repentance.

> Heavenly Father, would you please forgive me for foolishly trying to meet my own Core Needs in my own way. I am sorry that I have made bad choices like this in the past but I now realise that You, and You alone, are able to meet these needs for me in a way that nothing else, and no-one else, ever can. I repent of my self-centredness and my desire to be independent of You (I also repent of these other issues ...... (name them here) ....). I thank you that you sent Jesus to die for me so that the penalty for my sin could be paid in full. I ask You now to come into my life through The Holy Spirit to take control of my life and help me draw on Your divine resources for the future. I acknowledge Jesus Christ as my Saviour and Lord. I ask you to make me strong in these very areas and enable me to bring my life into line with Your eternal purposes. I ask this in Jesus name.
> Amen

AN EXAMPLE OF A PRAYER OF CONFESSION AND REPENTANCE

There will be those clients who may not be ready to accept that God alone can provide the answer to their core needs and will want to continue to try to meet their own needs in their own ways. Therefore at every step, the counsellor must point out the alternatives, along with their associated consequences, whilst still making it clear that the client is free to make their own choices. It may mean that it will be necessary to return to the spiritual circle on a number of occasions as the therapy continues, but on every occasion it must be the client's prerogative to make their own choices. It will be a great challenge to any counsellor to continue to work with a client who still wishes to trust in their own version of spirituality rather than to trust God. However, it is not unusual for a client to re-think such a decision as the process of working through the other circles continues, or even after the counselling has finished. Never give up hope because God will never abandon them.

THE RATIONAL CIRCLE RESOLUTIONS

The goal in this circle is to assist the client to change every problem-causing thought and irrational belief by bringing them into harmony with the Word of God. Foolish thinking amounts to anything that is inconsistent with the Word of God and is based on the wrong assumptions which come from our carnal nature. The process must begin here with the client specifically re-stating each dysfunctional belief and every negative thought which sustains it, as he identified during the Investigation Phase. The client is then encouraged to spot the lies which are contained in these statements and recognise how they contradict the Scriptures. Every lie must then be vigorously disputed, counteracted, and re-stated using truths from The Bible. For this to be effective, it is essential that the client is an active and enthusiastic participant in this process.

It is likely that as this exercise is being done by the client, lots of encouragement from the counsellor will be needed. <u>It must not be done for them</u>. Additional games, exercises and prescriptions can be introduced at this point which might help with the process and be a means of helping to sharpen the client's awareness. The client should be encouraged to repeat these exercises several times every day and become familiar with The Bible by looking up, writing down, memorising and meditating on each key verse for himself. In this way he will begin to establish a positive habit and build a personal resource that can be accessed at any time in the future. It may be necessary to stay in this stage for several counselling sessions until the client has a clear grasp of how to change his dysfunctional thinking and develop a right belief system. Once the client's thinking and beliefs have been brought into line with the principles of Scripture, he is ready to move on into the next circle.

THE VOLITIONAL CIRCLE RESOLUTIONS

The challenge now is to encourage the client to bring his choices into line with his new-found Biblical thinking and to set himself appropriate targets and goals which will enable him to move forward in a positive way. We want to encourage our clients to be single minded about this because The Bible explains that a double minded man is unstable in everything he does (James 1 v 8). It must be stressed once again that, although we all have the ability to exercise our freewill, within certain limits, we do not have the freedom to determine the consequences of our choices.

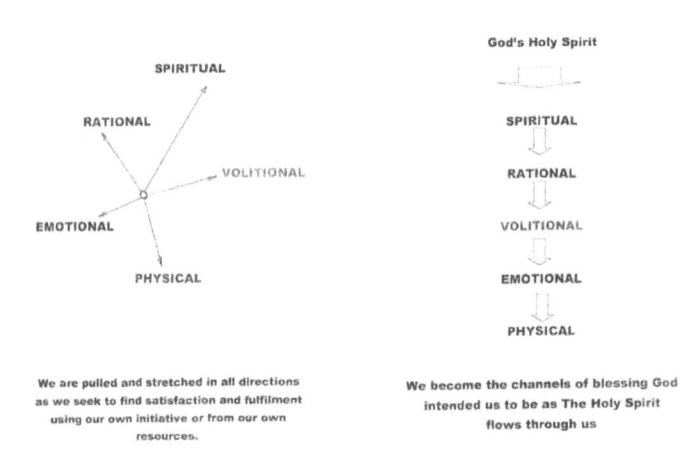

We are pulled and stretched in all directions as we seek to find satisfaction and fulfilment using our own initiative or from our own resources.

We become the channels of blessing God intended us to be as The Holy Spirit flows through us

"Before and After".

Looking at the linear diagram of the five elements of human functioning we can see that the Volitional phase is the pivot point of the whole process. If we make our choices on the basis of Spiritual and Rational principles these are more likely to be healthy and wholesome rather than choices based on Emotional and Physical factors which are more likely to keep us locked into negative and dysfunctional attitudes and behaviours. It is vital, therefore, to get our Spiritual and Rational functions in line with the way The Bible tells us we have been designed. This will enable us to make 'right' choices in the Volitional circle.

Psychologically, all behavioural responses are motivated by a chosen goal. This means, our verbal and emotional responses as well as our behaviours are all the result of the choices we make. The significant function in this circle, therefore, is to encourage the client to set goals for themselves that are in line with their new-found Biblical thinking and beliefs. Clients may struggle to accept that their behaviours are all a matter of choice because they will have been conditioned to believe the way they behave is perfectly normal for them. This emphasises the principle that making a change towards Godly behaviour can only happen by adopting Godly goals which are based on Godly thinking and Godly beliefs. When these are in place it is easier to make the choice to behave (respond) in a way that is consistent with these truths.

All behaviour is moving towards a goal and all goals are a matter of personal choice. This means that all behaviours are a matter of personal choice and therefore all behaviours can be changed – there are no exceptions. The biggest difficulty with this is to be willing to make such a change by learning to be obedient to The Word of God even when we don't feel like it. Goals which are based on our own selfish desires will always be prone to be sabotaged in some way and this will produce within us some powerful negative responses such as Anger, Anxiety, Fear and Guilt. The counsellor must now work with his client to encourage the development of positive, constructive goals that are in line with Godly principles in order to generate positive, healthy emotions and behaviours. To put it simply, the best goal will be that of pleasing The Lord because this is always achievable.

As the counsellor looks back at the notes he made from the Investigation Phase he will be able to help the client review his own responses to see how these were his own choice and were based on his own inappropriate goals. It may be worth spending some time at this point to help the client with some goal setting tools. Using the widely accepted SMART framework can be a really good place to start. Each goal should be:

Specific – clearly stated and broken down into its smallest constituent parts

Measurable – with quantifiable stages and markers for regular review

Appropriate – completely relevant to the overall direction and destination

Realistic – within the person's capabilities and available resources

Time Related – within an acceptable period and with a specific end.

These steps will increase the likelihood of successful achievement and improve the client's sense of progress. There are many other tools which may be useful to refine particular parts of the process such as: <u>The Force Field Analysis</u> which can help people to assess their motivation prior to embarking upon a course of action, or the <u>Decision Balance Sheet</u> which can create an understanding of the possible consequences prior to making a decision (see appendix). Using tools such as these, the counsellor might work with his client to help him develop a range of God-focused goals and be ready to move into the next circle.

THE EMOTIONAL CIRCLE RESOLUTIONS

The ability to handle negative emotions is often seen as a sign of spiritual maturity, so helping our clients to learn how to do this in a Godly fashion is the main objective in this circle. Learning how to control his emotions will also prevent the client from being controlled by them. Our emotions come from our evaluations, and our evaluations are formed from our knowledge and experience of life (see E+E=E diagram on page 55). There are a variety of ways in which we can handle our emotions, for example we can;

Express them – communicate, state, or demonstrate them openly
Repress them – restrict them, hold them in, deny or avoid them
Suppress them – eliminate them, put an end to, or prevent them
Confess them – acknowledge, admit and surrender them to God.

The greatest problems that arise from our emotions are the result of our unwillingness to adequately deal with the negative ones we have chosen to keep hidden. When we are unable to own them, admit to them and surrender them to God they will continue to reverberate and fester inside us with the potential to trigger mental and physical problems in the future. One mistake which unskilled therapists often make is to advise their clients to 'let it all out', to freely express their emotion or to take it out on another object. Punching a pillow to get rid of anger is a common example of this. However, they generally fail to realise that this form of expression serves only to reinforce the emotion. It can actually increase its intensity and does not resolve the problem.

At this point the counsellor must help his client see that the only sensible route to managing negative emotions is to confess them to God in an act of surrender and repentance. As he releases his feelings to God the client should ask The Lord to give him the strength, through The Holy Spirit, to receive supernatural healing and empowering in these very areas. Then, by reminding himself of the Godly choices and goals he selected in the Volitional circle, the client will be able to focus on managing his emotions more positively.

This can be a bit frightening for a client. The idea of digging up negative and painful emotions which the client has been denying or trying to keep buried can present a worrying challenge. The principle here is that it is impossible to give something to God (or anyone else) which you are not actually holding at the time. A common mistake here is to simply ask God to come and take them away. This rarely works because such action requires no personal involvement, apart from which, we cannot deal with anything that remains buried. We must first bring them to the surface. That means we must actually be holding and experiencing our difficult emotions before we can surrender them to God and receive His supernatural healing power.

THE PHYSICAL CIRCLE RESOLUTIONS

When a person is experiencing physical pain it is likely to affect every aspect of his ability to function, emotionally, volitionally, rationally and spiritually. In a similar manner, when there are unresolved problems in any of the other areas they are also likely to be contributory factors which will produce and/or sustain difficulties in the physical realm. In helping the client resolve his issues in the Physical Circle the counsellor must first of all take into account the issues that were highlighted in the Investigation Phase. Once each of the preceding circles have been adjusted and brought into line with Biblical principles, some of the physical issues may no longer be apparent. However, it is perfectly acceptable for a counsellor to encourage his client to seek a thorough medical check up in the case where he is experiencing persistent physical problems.

There are many physiological problems which can be caused by chemical and hormonal imbalances in a person's system so clients should never be discouraged from taking medication that has been prescribed by their medical specialist. Some conditions which could be diagnosed as deep emotional problems can actually be caused by the body not working as it should. The counsellor should be willing to spend time at this point encouraging his client to consider ways in which he might improve his physical health in line with Biblical principles. This might require the client to give prompt attention to addressing any such deficiencies, to address any destructive habits, or to commit to the adoption of a more healthy lifestyle. Steps like these will massively improve the client's chances of preventing any illnesses and ailments from gaining a habitual foothold and can result in great peace of mind.

FIVE CIRCLE SUMMARY

Once each of the circles of human functioning has been brought into line with Biblical principles, the client has the opportunity to become a channel of God's blessing to others. When the blockages are removed and The Holy Spirit is allowed to flow freely through each area of a person's life, a whole new perspective begins to emerge. The person is able to see themselves having a more effective role in the lives of other people and making a more powerful contribution to the work of the kingdom of God.

The 5 major elements of the Christian

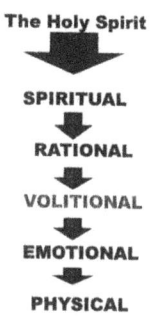

The Holy Spirit
⬇
SPIRITUAL
⬇
RATIONAL
⬇
VOLITIONAL
⬇
EMOTIONAL
⬇
PHYSICAL

THE FIVE ELEMENTS IN TOTAL HARMONY

As has been mentioned before, the Waverley Model is not meant to be a rigid format for counselling but one in which both counsellor and client can agree to be flexible and move from any one circle to another at any time throughout the process depending upon what is coming to the surface at that point. This makes it essential for the counsellor to keep comprehensive notes about what is being discussed and what is being agreed at each stage with the full cooperation and support of the client.

It is strongly recommend for counsellors to stress to their clients that to seek any psychological help from any other source whilst the current counselling relationship is in operation is completely unacceptable because this is likely to create confusion. As a general principle the client should be encouraged to wait until the counselling has come to a conclusion before seeking other help. However, it is appropriate to make an exception where the client may need professional help which does not interfere with his psychotherapy, for example, in the case where a client may require legal advice.

12

CONCLUSIONS

If any approach to counselling is to be called Christian it must first of all be based firmly on the foundational authority of The Bible. Then, if it is to be effective in helping people resolve their difficulties, it will also need to embrace the sound principles of psychology in a way that will help people discover a lasting sense of Security, Significance, and Self-Worth in their lives.

So why is it necessary to use a Christian approach to create a pathway towards excellence? Firstly because it is only when a process is used which looks at, and works with, every facet of the whole person, including their spiritual dimension, will it be possible for anyone to get to the source of each of their problematic issues. You see, the root cause of the majority of the issues with which people really struggle will always lie within their spiritual dimension and the spiritual dimension is best understood by studying the way our Maker has put us together. Secondly, it is only when the source of each problematic issue is exposed, brought to the surface and tackled, that any lasting benefit can be achieved and this is best done by applying the recommendations of the Maker as recorded in The Bible.

Of course, The Bible speaks specifically about God and the kind of relationship He wants to have with us, so there will be some people who will be put off by any direct references to using The Bible like this. The fact is, whether we believe it or not and whether we like it or not, we have all been created in the image of Almighty God, so there is no higher authority from which we can learn how to correct any dysfunctional areas that occur in our lives. Even the strongest of sceptics are going to be surprised when they discover this reality for themselves, but this can only happen as they begin to apply the principles of Christian counselling when working with properly qualified Christian counsellors.

In every area of life, the best resource for dealing with any problems which relate to something highly technical is always to consult the maker's instructions.

"See to it that no-one takes you captive through hollow and deceptive philosophy which depends on human tradition and the basic principles of this world, rather than on Christ" (Colossians 2 v 8).

In order to be ethically correct <u>and</u> spiritually correct therefore, we must adopt an approach to counselling that will effectively combine both the psychological and spiritual elements without compromise and will be in the best interests of our clients. This means that any overemphasis of either one of these elements to the exclusion of the other, could be considered to be a serious issue of malpractice. In addition, any attempt to use any counselling session merely as an opportunity to evangelise must be seen as something that is totally inappropriate and unacceptable in the counselling environment. However, a failure to bring the client's spiritual needs into the counselling process, and address them in an appropriate manner, must be seen to be equally unacceptable and a clear dereliction of duty.

To be equipped to work in this fashion will demand a high level of professionalism in both these elements and this is where Dr Larry Crabb suggests some specific standards which should be met before people could consider calling themselves Christian counsellors. He says:

1. Counsellors should accept psychological insights only if these are wholly consistent with Biblical truth.
2. Counsellors should regard The Bible as the infallible Word of God.
3. Counsellors should agree that Biblical principles will be put into practice consistently and will always take precedence over non-biblical principles.
4. Counsellors should be engaged in regular study of The Bible and be active members of a Bible-believing church.

(Adapted from Crabb, cited in Anderson 2000 p67)

He further believed that Christian Counsellors should be those who are willing to exercise the gifts of The Holy Spirit in an appropriate manner throughout the counselling relationship. However, although these elements may satisfy the Christian requirement, I do not believe these qualities to be sufficient on their own. Three other elements are essential for everyone who wishes to be identified as a counsellor, whether they are Christian or not: (i) they should have a practical understanding and appreciation of a variety of psychological approaches, (ii) they should choose to make themselves fully accountable through regular high quality counselling supervision, and (iii) they should agree to adhere to a nationally accepted code of ethics.

For counsellors to choose to call themselves 'Christian', or even to say that they work to Christian standards, is clearly not sufficient evidence of their ability to work effectively in this way. There can be no doubt that there are those who like to call themselves Christian counsellors but who lack adequate training and experience in either Counselling, understanding The Bible, knowledge of Psychology, or any combination of these. It is essential too, for them to see training and experience as an on-going requirement rather than something which may have been accomplished in the past. A commitment to Continuing Professional Development (CPD) must be an essential aspect of every counsellor's agenda. Whenever a counsellor believes they have 'arrived', or decides they need no further training, supervision or monitoring, it is time for them to give up immediately. They become potentially quite dangerous and should be avoided by anyone seeking counselling.

It is the integration of the spiritual (or our relationship to God) into the whole therapeutic process that sets Christian counselling apart from all forms of secular therapy (Anderson 2000), but it is essential for this to be done in a gentle, caring manner and with all the skill of a qualified practitioner. The process should always include a thorough explanation by the counsellor of every proposed step to be undertaken and an acknowledgement from the client that they understand and agree to proceed on this basis. Regardless of which forms of counselling and psychotherapy are being used, in order for them to be most effective they must be conducted at all times in a completely open and transparent manner. No aspect should ever appear to be secretive. Every client should understand how each aspect, especially the spiritual elements, fit together as part of the whole, and they should be encouraged to ask any questions they wish, at any time, as the relationship progresses.

If these standards are to be accepted as a foundation, we must now consider, for the Christian counsellor, the practicalities of how they actually make use of their Christian faith alongside psychological principles without compromising the counselling relationship. The counsellors who are most effective in doing this Neil Anderson calls 'Conjoint Counsellors'. He says:

> "they utilise explicit expressions of the spiritual aspects of life in a treatment plan, along with psychological assessment and treatment techniques to accomplish multi-dimensional goals with their clients" (Anderson 2000 p71).

With this in mind, there are some legitimate concerns about how and when it is appropriate to make use of the Scriptures, of prayer, and of the ministry of The Holy Spirit without jeopardising an ethical counselling relationship. It must never be assumed that these can simply be introduced at any point just because the counsellor is working from a Christian perspective, even if the client requests this. If the professional quality of the relationship is to be maintained, counselling protocols must be observed at all times. On the other hand, the use of the Scriptures, of prayer, and of the gifts of The Holy Spirit should not have to be confined purely within the discussions around the client's Spiritual realm. The counsellor should be able to introduce these naturally and spontaneously at any stage of the process provided the approval of the client has already been obtained through an open and frank discussion of what this might entail.

There have been many occasions when people have described to me how a 'counsellor' has quoted verses from The Bible to them or simply decided to pray for them without explaining how this fits into the counselling process. It can then appear to be a means of trying to make a point, or to convince them of the error of their ways or trying to coerce them into some course of action. Whilst this may be appropriate behaviour in lots of church situations it is quite unacceptable conduct for a counselling relationship.

It is really important for every Christian Counsellor to learn how to use The Bible effectively with their clients so as to increase their desire to know more and to develop a genuine desire to research and explore things for themselves. It is equally important for clients to be encouraged to discover the power of prayer, to develop their personal relationship with God, and to learn how to draw on the resources of The Holy Spirit for themselves. When this respect for the autonomy of the client is consistently demonstrated by the counsellor it will always serve to strengthen the bond between them. I am a great believer in the value of preaching and teaching but the counselling relationship must be one of exploration, discovery and application in a personal manner for every client. Counsellors would do well to remember and apply this maxim:

What we are told can soon fade, but what we discover for ourselves we rarely forget.

When it comes to the matter of prayer, every Christian counsellor should be regularly praying for their clients in their own time, but be extremely careful to use only appropriate ways of praying during the counselling sessions. As a general guide, it is best to think of prayer as something that is the client's prerogative within the sessions and is not the function of the counsellor, otherwise prayer can come across as a way of putting pressure on the client. There is great value to be gained by helping clients to realise they can draw on the resources of Almighty God with their own words and that this can be incredibly empowering for them.

Even people who have grown up under Christian influences may be surprised that they can have a personal relationship with God in this way and that they don't need someone else to do this for them. Some clients will be happy to immediately respond to this approach when asked, whereas others will need a lot of encouragement and help before they feel comfortable about praying in front of you. Encouraging clients to bring their own issues to God, in their own words, is a way of helping them discover and develop their own effective way to offload their worries and anxieties. It is a way of helping them tap into the resources of God whilst still respecting their freedom and autonomy.

What makes Christian counselling really effective is not just to do with combining the spiritual and psychological elements, it is about adopting a comprehensive approach to the whole person by understanding how all the constituent parts can be contributing to the problem and, how all the constituent parts can become part of the resolution. If counsellors become so desperate to see some improvement in their clients that they fall into the trap of focusing on symptom relief instead of getting to the source of the problems, they are in danger of trivialising their clients issues and then unwittingly helping to perpetuate the opinion that counselling really doesn't work. When God spoke to deceitful prophets through Jeremiah, He accused them in this way;

"They dress the wound of my people as though it were not serious"
(Jeremiah 6 v 14 and again in Jeremiah 8 v 11)

What is meant by this accusation is that they were not getting to the source of the problems because they were too concerned about keeping up appearances and meeting their own needs. He called this deceit. What God had said earlier applied both to the prophets and to their hearers, that people had committed only two sins: firstly they had ignored Him along with all the resources He was making available to them which would satisfy their needs, and secondly they had chosen to trust in their own resources and abilities which were inherently flawed and would never provide the satisfaction they craved (Jeremiah 2 v 13). The root cause of practically every major problem we face in this life falls into one of these two categories.

We need to understand that all the deep internal drives that are common to man can only be fully met as we make the choice to live according to the standards God has set out for us, and this only becomes possible when we have a personal encounter with Jesus. Christian counsellors will inevitably come across many people who will be unable or unwilling to accept this, but our belief in the Word of God must not falter. Our foundation must remain solid at all times and take us to the immovable and unshakable rock on which our counselling practice is firmly grounded – the person of the living Lord Jesus Christ.

Christian counselling is like living the Christian Life, it works best when it is an ongoing partnership of exploration and discovery. As we partner with our clients however, we must never allow our major emphasis to become a desire to change them for this is the sole prerogative of The

Holy Spirit and if we try to take this over, we will inevitably get in His way and hinder the whole process. Our desire must always be focused on looking for that sense of relief, excitement and joy that comes to our clients when they make their own life-changing discoveries either from the practical application of these principles, or directly from the Word of God. We then stand to get an immense thrill when we witness them beginning to make healthy and constructive decisions about the future which are based on their new-found discoveries. This is our reward and it is what keeps us going through the hard times because it is the very essence of becoming a Christian counsellor.

APPENDICES

1. The Counselling Contract

The Counselling Contract

Here is a selection of topics which need to be covered at some stage in the counselling relationship. These must never become rules or be presented in a dictatorial fashion, but should be presented in a manner that seeks to put the client completely at ease and answer some possible concerns even before they arise.

1. **Counsellor's identity / Agency**
2. **Competence – Training, Qualifications etc**
3. **Code of Ethics and Practice**
4. **Confidentiality and possible main exceptions**
5. **Counselling Process – Main Approach, Notes**
6. **Content - Focus purely on Client's issues**
7. **Conditions - Alcohol, Other counselling etc**
8. **Costs and How to Pay**
9. **Commitment – Timings, Assignments etc**
10. **Consultancy and/or Supervision**
11. **Client Reviews of Progress**
12. **Cancellations – by Client and/or Counsellor**
13. **Complaints Procedure and how to Access**
14. **Clarification - Client's Questions**
15. **Counselling Evaluation and Ending**

It may be unrealistic to present all these topics before any counselling begins, so choices about the timing of each topic may be significant.

TRS/C/09/08

2. The Decision Balance Sheet

Decision Balance Sheet

If I choose to ....

GAINS	LOSSES
SELF	
SIGNIFICANT OTHERS	
SOCIAL CONTACTS	

TRS/C/04/94

3. The Force Field Analysis

Force Field Analysis

IDENTIFIABLE GOAL	
INTERNAL	**EXTERNAL**
Hinders: Thoughts / Feelings / Limitations	Hinders: People / Finance / Conditions
Helps: Determination / Skills / Resources	Helps: People / Timing / Environment

TRS/C/01/09

4. The Growth Model of Coaching

Christian Coaching and Mentoring (CCAM)

GROWTH Model

Identify **G**OAL(S) (What do you want to achieve?)

Establish by discussion about hopes, dreams, visions, ideals, wishes, thoughts etc. Tie them down very specifically. Create actual and mental pictures and descriptions based on Biblical principles.

Assess **R**EALITY (What is the current situation?)

Consider the actual circumstances and situations in assessing the likelihood of possible achievement. Discuss resources, finance, equipment, materials etc that would be required. Use the Decision Balance Sheet (DBS).

Review **O**PTIONS (What could you do?)

Outline existing Strengths, Skills, Abilities, Contacts and Resources. Work through a SWOT analysis. Use the Force Field Analysis Sheet (FFA) to look at all possible pathways going forward.

Action **W**AY FORWARD (How will you tackle the issue?)

Utilise a clear action plan, broken down into its smallest constituent parts with manageable steps and time frames. Build in checks and monitoring processes with accountability at every stage.

Develop **T**ACTICS (What approaches will ensure success?)

Prepare a personal strategy for attacking each step in the process. Plan to make even the breaks and hold-ups constructive times. Build-in periods for advice, relaxation, encouragement and refreshment.

Build **H**ABITS (How will you sustain success?)

Construct a programme of regular positive activity and thinking, including on-going personal development, that will continue to transform the ways in which all forms of challenges can be faced in the future.

Adapted from Growth Coaching International (Australia)   TRS/CCAM/ 09/16

5. The Process of Forgiveness

FORGIVENESS

1. I need to know God's forgiveness for all my sin.

Thank you Lord Jesus for dying so that I might be forgiven. Thank you that the sacrifice you made for me was perfect and complete in every way. Thank you that you have paid the price for my sin in full and this opens the way for me to receive complete forgiveness. I do not deserve this forgiveness and can never earn it by anything I do, but I want to receive it now because you promise in The Bible that this is available to me. Please forgive me for all the sin in my life (everything I've done which is not in accordance with your standards and principles), I am truly sorry and really want to be completely different. I ask you to cleanse me and wash me and help me to turn from my selfish ways and become the person you designed me to be. Thank you Jesus.

2. I need to forgive all those who have ever hurt me.

Thank you Jesus for forgiving me. Pease help me now to be able to forgive all those who have hurt me in any way whatsoever. By an act of my will I now choose to express the desire of my heart to forgive all those who have hurt me and to be free of this bondage for ever. (Now simply name each person and give them over to God). Jesus, I release each of these people into the freedom of my forgiveness because of what you have already done for me on the cross at Calvary. As I release them to you in simple obedience to your Word, I receive your supernatural healing power into these areas of my life. Please help me never to pick up this hurt again.

3. I need to ask for the forgiveness of those I have wronged.

Lord Jesus please help me to make contact with every person I have wronged and ask them to forgive me. Please give me the humility and strength I will need and help me to do this in a way that brings honour to you regardless of how it is received. I wish to bring nothing but love and blessing into their lives. (Now decide on an appropriate course of action for each person, eg; a letter, a telephone call, a visit, etc., and ask The Lord to guide you as you prepare.)

4. I need to ask God to forgive me when I've blamed Him.

Father I confess that in the past I have blamed you for things as if you didn't care about me or were being deliberately nasty to me. I recognise this as a sin and ask you to forgive me. I know that you hate what satan has done in my life, but I thank you that you love me and promise to set me free. (Now confess and name these specific areas - eg; Barrenness, Singleness, Illness, Inherited traits, problems or Disasters).

5. I need to forgive myself.

Thank you Father for promising me complete forgiveness in every area of my life. I now need to be able to forgive myself for all the things for which you have already forgiven me and to release myself from the bondage of my own judgements. I now exercise my will and choose to forgive myself through the precious blood of Jesus Christ my Lord and my Saviour.

"If we confess our sins, He is faithful and just and will forgive us our sins and purify us from all unrighteousness" 1 John 1 v 9.

TRS/CC/07/03

6. The Cognitive Principles of Schema

The Cognitive Principle of Schema

A Schema is an extremely stable and enduring pattern of responses that usually, but not always, develops during childhood or early life and which is strengthened, developed and reinforced through the experiences of life. We generally manage our world through our Schemas.

Schemas are:

- Unconditional
- Usually not available to the consciousness
- Latent, and can be active or dormant according to the presence or absence of the relevant triggers
- Neither 'good' nor 'bad', and may be functional or dysfunctional according to the client's experiences and goals
- Compelling or Non-compelling to the extent in which they are active and influential
- Pervasive and Narrow
- Deeply ingrained

The Major Schemas can be identified as:

1. Emotional Deprivation,   2. Abandonment,   3. Mistrust / Abuse,

4. Social Isolation,   5. Defectiveness / Shame,   6. Social Undesirability,

7. Failure to Achieve,   8. Functional Dependence / Incompetence,

9. Vulnerability to Harm,   10. Enmeshment,   11. Subjugation,

12. Self Sacrifice,   13. Emotional Inhibition,   14. Unrelenting Standards,

15. Entitlement,   16. Insufficient Control / Discipline.

Adapted from 'Lifetraps' by Jeffery Young (1990)

7. A Client Risk Assessment Form

POSITIVE RELEASE RISK ASSESSMENT   Client No. ......

1. **Current Feelings**
   Feelings about the Future
   Levels of Hopelessness   **Assessments**

                                                             (i) .... ☐

2. **Any significant thoughts about Self Harm**

                                                             (ii) .... ☐

3. **Suicide Plan**

                                                             (iii) .... ☐

4. **History of Previous Attempts**

                                                             (iv) .... ☐

5. **Particular Stressors**

                                                             (v) .... ☐

6. **Current Symptoms**

7. **Alcohol &/or Drug Use**

                                                             Action Taken

8. **Psychiatric/Medical History**

                                                             GP

9. **Current Support Network**   Other

10.   **GP / CPN Contact Details etc.**   Follow Up

                                                             Further Action Req'd

1 = Serious,   2 = Moderate,   3 = Small,   4 = None Apparent

8. A Client Assessment of Psychological Progress

CAPP   **CLIENT QUESTIONNAIRE**   **1**

Client Assessment of Psychological Progress

Client .... No. .... Client Assessment ....

Referred by: ....

1. Choose one part of your condition which troubles you the most ....

    .... (Therapist assessment) ....

    a) Rate how much this has affected you over the past 7 days

        Good 1   2   3   4   5   6   7   8   9   10 Bad

    b) How long ago were you first concerned about this ....

2. Choose another part of your condition that troubles you ....

    .... (Therapist assessment) ....

    a) Rate how much this has affected you over the past 7 days

        Good 1   2   3   4   5   6   7   8   9   10 Bad

    b) How long ago were you first concerned about this aspect ....

3. Choose one thing that, because of these problems, it has been hard for you to do over the past 7 days ....

    Rate how hard this has been for you over the past 7 days

        Good 1   2   3   4   5   6   7   8   9   10 Bad

4. Choose another thing that, because of these problems, has been hard for you to do over the past 7 days ....

    Rate how hard this has been for you over the past 7 days

        Good 1   2   3   4   5   6   7   8   9   10 Bad

5. Rate how you have felt about yourself generally over the past 7 days

        Good 1   2   3   4   5   6   7   8   9   10 Bad

Signed (Client) .... (Therapist) .... Date ....

CAPP

CLIENT REVIEW FORM

2

Client Assessment of Psychological Progress

Client .... No. .... Actual Issues ....

Focus of the Work: ....

....

.... Total No. Sessions ....

1. This is the part of your condition which you said troubled you the most
   ....

   Rate how much this has affected you over the past 7 days

   Good 1   2   3   4   5   6   7   8   9   10 Bad

2. This is another part of your condition that you said troubled you
   ....

   Rate how much this has affected you over the past 7 days

   Good 1   2   3   4   5   6   7   8   9   10 Bad

3. This is one thing you said was hard to do because of these problems
   ....

   Rate how hard it has been for you to do this over the past 7 days

   Good 1   2   3   4   5   6   7   8   9   10 Bad

4. This is another thing you said was hard to do because of these problems
   ....

   Rate how hard it has been for you to do this over the past 7 days

   Good 1   2   3   4   5   6   7   8   9   10 Bad

5. Rate how you have felt about yourself generally over the past 7 days

   Good 1   2   3   4   5   6   7   8   9   10 Bad

6. Please identify any issues that you still wish to discuss with your counsellor
   ....
   ....

Signed (Client) .... (Therapist) .... Date ....

TRS/CC/06/05

9. A Counselling Supervision Programme

SUPERVISION

Good supervision ensures that counsellors work ethically and competently, and serves as a safeguard for counsellors experiencing difficulties in their work.

The Main Components

1. To support and encourage the counsellor
2. To teach the counsellor to integrate theoretical knowledge and practice
3. To assess the maintenance of counselling standards
4. To transmit professional values and ethics
5. To help the counsellor develop through insight and reflection
6. To enable the counsellor to develop skills and build self-confidence
7. To help the counsellor identify and share vulnerabilities
8. To assist with the counsellor's disappointments and limitations
9. To help the counsellor move forward with a stuck client
10. To get counsellors to evaluate their work and effectiveness
11. To share ideas and explore different counselling approaches
12. To report on the client's progress or lack of progress
13. To recharge the counsellor's batteries
14. To review the counsellor's work load and time management
15. To be part of the continuing personal development of the counsellor
16. To encourage appropriate records to be maintained
17. To help the counsellor balance work with other responsibilities

Three Main Approaches

1. Focus on the Case. This involves primarily looking at the problem a client has brought to counselling in order to assist the counsellor to find ways of helping the client to move forward.
2. Focus on the Counsellor. This concentrates on the feelings of the counsellor as the issues of the client unfold and encourages the use of more empathic responses throughout the process.
3. Focus on the Communication. This seeks to reveal similarities between the 'supervision' and the 'counselling' processes which give insight into the effectiveness of the counsellor's work.

Adapted from "Learning to Counsel" by Sutton and Stewart (2002)

TRS/C/08/03

REFERENCES AND BIBLIOGRAPHY

1. Adams J.E. (1970) — *Competent to Counsel* — Zondervan. Grand Rapids
2. Adams J.E. (1973) — *The Christian Counsellor's Manual* — Zondervan. Grand Rapids
3. Adams J.E. (1986) — *Insight and Creativity in Christian Counselling* — Zondervan. Grand Rapids
4. Altman R. (1996) — *Counselling in the Community* — Kingsway. Eastbourne
5. Anderson N. & Goss S. (2007) — *The Freedom in Christ Discipleship Course* — Monarch Books. Oxford
6. Anderson N. & Zeuhlke T. (2000) — *Christ-Centred Therapy* — Zondervan. Grand Rapids
7. Ashley O. (2017) — *The Bible, Wisdom, and Human Nature* — CWR. Farnham
8. Beck A. T. (1976) — *Cognitive Therapy and the Emotional Disorders* — Penguin. New York
9. Benner D.G. (Ed) (1987) — *Christian Counselling and Psychotherapy* — Baker Bookhouse. Grand Rapids
10. Bloom W. (2011) — *The Power of Modern Spirituality* — Piatkus. London
11. Bridger F. & Atkinson D. (1994) — *Counselling in Context* — Harper Collins. London
12. Capps D. (1981) — *Biblical Approaches to Pastoral Counselling* — Westminster Pub Co. Philadelphia
13. Clebsh W. & Jaekle C. (1964) — *Pastoral Care in Historical Perspective* — Harper Torchbooks. New York
14. Clinton T. & Hawkins R. (2009) — *Biblical Counselling* — Baker Books. Grand Rapids
15. Clinton T. & Hawkins R. (2011) — *The Popular Encyclopedia of Christian Counselling* — Harvest House. Oregon
16. Clinton T. & Straub J. (2010) — *God Attachment: why you believe, act and feel* — Howard Books. New York

17.	Cloud H & Townsend J. (1992)	*Boundaries: when to say Yes, and when to say No*	Zondervan. Grand Rapids
18.	Cogley J. (2018)	*Wood You Believe: the spiritual self*	Rotomail Italia SpA. Vignate (MI)
19.	Collins G. R. (1989)	*Christian Counselling – a comprehensive guide.*	Word (UK) Ltd. Milton Keynes
20.	Collins Dictionary (2009)	*Collins English Dictionary Home Edition*	Harper Collins. Glasgow
21.	Corey G. (1991)	*The Theory and Practice of Counselling and Psychotherapy*	Brooks Cole. California
22.	Crabb L.J. (1989)	*Basic Principles of Biblical Counselling*	Marshall Pickering. London
23.	Culliford L. (2011)	*The Psychology of Spirituality*	Kingsley. London
24.	Dorricott K. (2014)	*Christian Counseling*	Amazon. GB
25.	Feltham C. & Horton I. (2000)	*Handbook of Counselling and Psychotherapy*	Sage. London
26.	Fontana D. (2003)	*Psychology, Religion and Spirituality*	BPS Blackwell. Oxford
27.	Frankl V. E. (1967)	*Man's Search for Meaning*	Beacon Books. Boston
28.	Frankl V. E. (1988)	*The Will to Meaning*	Meridian Books. Illinois
29.	Frankl V. E. (2011)	*Man's Search for Ultimate Meaning*	Rider Books. New York
30.	Freeman A & Greenwood V (1987)	*Cognitive Therapy – in Psychiatric & Medical Settings*	Human Sciences Press. New York
31.	Ganz R. (1993)	*Psychobabble: the failure of modern psychology*	Crossway Books. Illinois
32.	Gross R. D. (1992)	*Psychology – The Science of the Mind and Behaviour*	Hodder & Stoughton. Sevenoaks
33.	Harborne L. (2011)	*Working with Issues of Spirituality, Faith, Religion or Belief*	BACP Information Sheet No. G13
34.	Hawkins R. & Clinton T. (2015)	*The New Christian Counsellor*	Harvest House. Oregon
35.	Hough M. (1994)	*A Practical Approach to Counselling*	Pitman Publishing. London
36.	Hurding R.F. (1982)	*Christian Care and Counselling*	Morehouse-Barlow Co. Connecticut
37.	Johnson E.L. & Jones S.L. (2000)	*Psychology and Christianity*	Inter Varsity Press. Illinois
38.	Jones S.L. & Butman R.E. (2011)	*Modern Psychotherapies*	Inter Varsity Press. Illinois
39.	Kallmier R. (2011)	*Caring and Counselling: an introduction to the Waverley model*	CWR. Farnham
40.	Knabb J.J. et al (2019)	*Christian Psychotherapy in Context*	Routledge. New York
41.	Knox R. et al (2013)	*Relational Depth: new perspectives and developments*	Palgrave MacMillan. New York

42.	Langdridge D. (2007)	*Phenomenological Psychology*	Pearson Educ. Harlow
43.	Ledger P. (1989)	*Counselling and The Holy Spirit*	Marshall Pickering. London
44.	Lyall D. (1985)	*Counselling in the Pastoral and Spiritual Context*	Open Univ Press. Buckingham
45.	Marlatt G. & Gordon J. (Eds) (1985)	*Relapse Prevention: maintenance strategies*	Guilford Press. New York
46.	McMinn M.R. (1991)	*Cognitive Therapy Techniques in Christian Counselling*	Word Publishing. Dallas
47.	McMinn M.R. (1996)	*Psychology, Theology and Spirituality*	Tyndale House. Illinois
48.	Mearns D. & Cooper M. (2005)	*Working at Relational Depth*	Sage. London
49.	Mearns D. & Thorne B. (1999)	*Person-Centred Counselling in Action*	Sage. London
50.	Mearns D. & Thorne B. (2007)	*Person-Centred Therapy Today*	Sage. London
51.	Meier P.D. et al (1991)	*Introduction to Psychology and Counselling*	Monarch Pubs. Tunbridge Wells
52.	Miller W. & Rollnick S. (1991)	*Motivational Interviewing - preparing people to change*	Guilford Press. New York
53.	Nelson-Jones R. (2003)	*Basic Counselling Skills*	Sage. London
54.	Nelson-Jones R. (2003)	*Theory and Practice of Counselling & Therapy (3rd Ed)*	Sage. London
55.	Ogilvie L.J. (1995)	*The Greatest Counsellor in The World*	Vine Books. Michigan
56.	O'Hanlon B. & Beadle S. (1997)	*A Guide to Possibility Land*	Norton Books. New York
57.	O'Hanlon B. (2006)	*Pathways to Spirituality*	Norton Books. New York
58.	Peck A. (2014)	*Coaching and Mentoring: an introductory guide for Christians*	CWR. Farnham
59.	Peterson E. (1980)	*Who Cares ? a handbook of Christian Counselling*	Morehouse-Barlow Co. Connecticut
60.	Richards P.S. & Bergin A.E. (1997)	*A Spiritual Strategy for Counselling and Psychotherapy*	APA Books. Washington
61.	Rogers C. R. (1951)	*Client Centred Therapy*	Redwood Burn Ltd. Wiltshire
62.	Rogers C. R. (1961)	*On Becoming a Person*	Constable. London
63.	Rogers C.R. (1967)	*The Therapeutic Relationship and its Impact*	Univ of Wisconsin Press. Madison
64.	Rowan J. (2005)	*The Transpersonal: Spirituality in Psychotherapy*	Routledge. London
65.	Sanders P. (Ed) (2009)	*The Tribes of the Person-Centred Nation*	PCCS Books. Ross-on-Wye

66.	Simmons J. & Griffiths R (2009)	*CBT for Beginners*	Sage. London
67.	Spinelli E. (2007)	*Practising Existential Psychotherapy*	Sage. London
68.	Sutton J. & Stewart W. (2002)	*Learning to Counsel*	How To Books. Oxford
69.	Tan S-Y (2011)	*Counselling and Psychotherapy: a Christian Perspective*	Baker Books. Grand Rapids
70.	Van der Zanden J. W. (1977)	*Social Psychology*	Random House. New York
71.	van Deurzen E. (2002)	*Existential Counselling in Practice*	Sage. London
72.	van Deurzen E & Adams M (2017)	*Skills in Existential Counselling and Psychotherapy*	Sage. London
73.	Weishaar M. E. (1993)	*Aaron T. Beck*	Sage. London
74.	West W. (2000)	*Psychotherapy and Spirituality*	Sage. London
75.	West W. (2004)	*Spiritual Issues in Therapy*	Palgrave MacMillan. Basingstoke
76.	Wilber K. (2000)	*Integral Psychology*	Shambhala. Boston
77.	Yalom I. D. (1980)	*Existential Psychotherapy*	Basic Books. New York
78.	Yalom I. D. (2010)	*The Gift of Therapy*	Piatkus Books. London
79.	Young J E & Klosko J S (1994)	*Reinventing Your Life*	Penguin. New York

ABOUT THE AUTHOR

Trevor Summerlin has for over 35 years been the Principal of Positive Release. This is his own private practice dedicated to the very highest standards of Counselling, Psychotherapy, Training, Supervision, and Coaching, based on tried, tested and proven Christian principles.

Prior to this Trevor spent more than 20 years working in Outdoor Activities where he qualified as a BASI ski instructor, an English Ski Council Coach and a trainer in both Christian and secular Youthwork.

He gained experience in senior management and marketing in the leisure industry before being called into the Christian ministry. In addition to being a Baptist Pastor he established a Registered Charity, formed a Limited Company, opened a community shop, and ran an alcohol-free bar working with hundreds of teenagers every week.

He qualified as a Cognitive Therapy practitioner with a Masters Degree from the University of Wales on 'Stress in Leadership'. He later qualified as a Family Law Mediator, and as a professional Coach with Coaching and Mentoring International. He was appointed a Fellow of the Institute of Sales and Marketing Management in 1988, a Fellow of the Institute of Leadership and Management in 2006, and has been a registered member of the British Association for Counselling and Psychotherapy since 1996.

He has lectured on training courses in many colleges across South Wales including Cardiff and Vale College and the Open University. He has run Christian leadership courses, Seminars and Workshops for numerous churches and helped to establish a number of Christian Counselling Teams to serve their local community.

His on-going passion as a preacher and teacher is to help people understand that if they choose to apply the principles of The Bible in their everyday lives they will give themselves the very best chance of being successful at whatever they choose to do.

Trevor and his wife are based in South Wales, UK, where they are kept busy with Christian ministry, Christian Counselling, Writing, and taming their garden.

OTHER PUBLICATIONS BY THE SAME AUTHOR

A series of small booklets helping people towards Spiritual Maturity entitled **"Gateway to Life"**

1. Fundamentals
2. Moving Forward
3. Breaking Free
4. Understanding Holy Spirit
5. Exploring Worship
6. Christian Paradoxes
7. Spiritual Maturity

Available from the website www.gateway-to-life.info

"Christian Parallels"
A book which explores the similarities between learning to ski and living the Christian life.
ISBN: 978-1-913247-60-7
Published by Kingdom Publishers, Enfield, UK.
Widely available through bookshops

Lightning Source UK Ltd.
Milton Keynes UK
UKHW010638211021
392589UK00001B/75